The Ultimate Stock Picker's Guide

24 Top Experts Recommend 25 Stocks to Buy & Hold

The Ultimate Stock Picker's Guide

24 Top Experts Recommend 25 Stocks to Buy & Hold

Warren Boroson

IRWIN
Professional Publishing®
Chicago • London • Singapore

© Warren Boroson, 1996

This publication is designed to provide accurate and authoritative information in regard to the subject matter covered. It is sold with the understanding that neither the author nor the publisher is engaged in rendering legal, accounting, or other professional service. If legal advice or other expert assistance is required, the services of a competent professional person should be sought.

From a Declaration of Principles jointly adopted by a Committee of the American Bar Association and a Committee of Publishers.

Irwin Professional Book Team

Executive editor: *Kevin Commins*
Manging editor: *Kevin Thornton*
Senior marketing manager: *Tiffany Dykes*
Project editor: *Christina Thornton-Villagomez*
Production supervisor: *Pat Frederickson*
Assistant manager, desktop services: *Jon Christopher*
Manager, direct marketing: *Rebecca S. Gordon*
Designer: *Larry J. Cope*
Compositor: *The Publishing Services Group*
Typeface: *10.5/13 Palatino*
Printer: *Buxton Skinner Printing Company*

 Times Mirror
Higher Education Group

Library of Congress Cataloging-in-PublicationData

Boroson, Warren
    The ultimate stock picker's guide ; 24 top experts recommend 25
stocks to buy and hold / Warren Boroson.
        p.   cm.
    Includes index.
    ISBN 1-55738-823-7
    1. Stocks—United States.   I. Title.
HG4910.B67 1996
332.63'22—dc20   95-21277
                                                          CIP

Printed in the United States of America
 2 3 4 5 6 7 8 9 0 BS 2 1 0 9 8 7 6 5

Contents

Introduction

The focus of this book is on making a decent profit by investing in stocks.

It is, in fact, remarkably easy for people to make decent profits in the stock market. All you need do is create a stock portfolio by buying, over time, a diverse selection of excellent stocks, and holding on to them. In effect you create your own "unit investment trust (UIT)": a basket of securities that you normally never sell. Not last year's winners, or the stocks of tiny, promising companies, but the stocks of sound, conservative companies.

To help you choose stocks for your own unit investment trust, I asked a panel of 30 professional investors to identify good stocks for people to buy and hold. (Two investors answered the questionnaire as a team.) Twenty-four of them provided me with names, and all stocks that the panelists mentioned more than once are listed in Chapter 16, along with information about them, generously provided by the Standard & Poor's Corporation. (For a complete list of the stocks, see Appendix 2.)

The strategy of creating your own unit investment trust is identified with the well-known investor Warren Buffett, who buys, forever, the stocks of companies he wants to own. This strategy actually harks back to at least 1935, when a group of investors bought 30 blue-chip stocks that have since become the unit investment trust known as Lexington Corporate Leaders. That unit investment trust has done quite well indeed, without any supervision, without any turnover. Today only 23 stocks of the original 30 remain in the fund, but this very old-fashioned portfolio nonetheless seems to be thriving. As of this writing, Lexington Corporate Leaders receives five stars, the highest possible rating, from Morningstar, Inc. the Chicago-based research house (see Chapter 9).

Other simple, no-nonsense ways to prosper in the stock market are also described in this book. Among them: following the recommendations of a newsletter or paid professional (Chapter 1), buying the most miserable stocks in the Dow Jones Industrial Average (Chapter 4), investing in index funds (Chapter 8), and assembling a variety of mutual funds.

Yet it's also very easy for people *not* to make decent profits in the stock market—if like many investors, they own just a handful of this and that, and are prone to keeping losers while selling winners. (Or selling losers too late and selling winners too soon.) I've never seen, anywhere, a comprehensive list of all the possible reasons why so many investors manage to lose money in the stock market when it is so easy to make money—a gap that Chapter 2 attempts to fill.

If you do decide to create your own portfolio, whether a UIT or not, you should consider, among other things, how many different stocks you should own. The academics have one answer; our panelists had a different answer (see Chapter 6).

Don't be discouraged if many of your choices blow up in your face, either because of mistakes or because choosing good stocks happens to be a business fraught with peril. You may be surprised to learn how frequently even famous investors buy certain stocks . . . and rue the day (Chapter 7).

If you are to be successful in assembling your own portfolio, though, there is one principle you must follow: establish a strategy and stick with it (Chapter 10). One notable strategy is to buy the stocks of companies that seem undervalued. Another is to buy the stocks of companies whose earnings have been growing mightily and regularly. In examining the questionnaires that the panelists filled out, I discovered, to my surprise, that the differences between value and growth investors are far wider than I had known. The extent of these differences is not a subject that, to my knowledge, has been examined in depth (see Chapter 3).

Other chapters in the book present the panelists' responses to such questions as: Why should you buy a particular stock? When should you sell? How long might you typically hold the stocks you buy? What are the worst mistakes that even professional investors make? Do professional investors ever "market time," trying to avoid bear markets?

In many cases, the answers to these questions were sharply divergent, depending on whether the panelists were growth, value, or both growth and value investors. And in their strategies, even growth investors may differ markedly from other growth investors, and value investors from other value investors. This is to be expected, of course; it explains why some growth investors do better than others, and some value investors do better than others.

Finally, beginning investors or seasoned investors who want a refresher course on price/earning are referred to Appendix 1, which is a brief introduction to the subject of investing in the stock market. Readers' comments on this book would be welcome.

Warren Boroson
Glen Rock, New Jersey

Chapter 1

Six Ways to Invest in the Stock Market

At a memorable panel discussion in Washington, D.C., a number of years ago, three money managers described their markedly different methods of investing in the stock market. All had been successful; their portfolios, over the years, had averaged about an 18 percent gain a year.

One of the speakers was Philip Carret, a mere stripling of about 90 at the time. Carret, who turned 98 in 1994, had launched the Pioneer Funds of Boston in 1928.

Another speaker was Julian Lerner, who ran the AIM Constellation Fund—with unusual success—until he retired in 1994.

The third speaker was Max Heine, the gentle, witty man who guided the extraordinarily successful Mutual Series funds, now managed—with similar success—by Michael F. Price.

It was Heine who attempted to solve the mystery of why three different money managers, following different strategies, had all done so well. "All roads," he said, "lead to Jerusalem." (The man who had arranged the conference, William Lippman of the Templeton/Franklin funds, claims that Heine had actually said, "Almost all roads lead to Jerusalem." But that was not how I heard it.)

The message Heine was conveying was that it is not formidably difficult to make a profit in the stock market. And the stock market, for most people, is essentially what investing is about.

Unfortunately, many if not most investors choose the riskier ways to invest in the stock market instead of the safer ways.

The safer ways entail:

- Owning a basketful of different stocks in a variety of industries.
- Keeping those stocks for at least five years.

1

- Not selling them when stocks in general are depressed.
- Homing in on blue-chip stocks—those of old, prosperous corporations, like General Electric and Johnson & Johnson.

In fact, the single safest way to buy stocks is probably to buy shares of a diversified large-company stock index fund, one that owns so many different stocks in different industries that you are almost certain to keep pace with the stock market as a whole.

Anyone not much interested in investing, but of a mind to make money in the stock market conservatively, can just place money, at regular intervals, into Vanguard Index Total Stock Market, an index fund. The minimum first investment is $3,000; for subsequent invest-ments, the minimum is $500. Phone 1-800-662-7447 for a prospectus and an application. While there are other index funds available, none are more diversified than Vanguard Index Total Stock Market, which tracks the Wilshire 5000 (which has about 6,500 stocks), and very likely none have lower expenses.

There's nothing wrong with someone's not having much interest in investing and wanting more time to read novels, listen to music, work for voluntary organizations, or whatever. Anyone so inclined might proceed now to Chapter 8 on investing in index funds, then lend this book to someone else.

Investing in an index fund might be dismissed as a "no brainer," but there is no question that the great majority of stock market investors would be far better off investing in a single, diversified index fund than in their current messy portfolios.

The riskiest way to invest in stocks is what many people seem to do: to buy four or six stocks without much rhyme or reason—on tips from friends or from the press, or at the suggestion of their stock-brokers—then to manage their own portfolios, with or without the guidance of their stockbrokers.

Investing on your own can be rewarding—if you have the time, the interest, and the skill. But the odds are against you. Killings in the stock market by amateur investors are typically aberrations.

I once met a truculent gentleman, at a conference of the National Association of Investment Clubs, who told me that every single stock that he had ever bought had made him money. When I passed that boast along to an investment professional, his reply was: "Anyone who never loses money in the stock market isn't taking enough chances."

(Another good answer would have been: Anyone who hasn't lost money in stocks hasn't been investing very long.)

In 1994, for example, a big to-do was made about 16 women from Beardstown, Illinois, average age 63.5, whose investment record had given them an average return of 23 percent a year. But if you actually read the book they had written, you would have learned, first of all, that the women knew little about investing. And, second, that their success was almost entirely due to their following the recommendations in the newsletter, *The Value Line Investment Survey*. (Value Line's recommended stocks have a long history of doing exceptionally well—and confounding advocates of the efficient-market theory, the view that all stocks are always reasonably priced. Mark Hulbert, editor of *The Hulbert Financial Digest*, has been tracking the performances of investment newsletters for years. He has found that *The Value Line Investment Survey* has been the single most profitable.)

In between those two extremes of investing—the diversified index fund and the messy neglected portfolio—are a few other major strategies that an investor might consider.

You need not, after all, limit yourself to one strategy. You could, for example, own a diversified index fund along with individual stocks, or along with actively managed mutual funds.

A step down from the safety of a diversified stock index fund is a unit investment trust of stocks. A UIT is a collection of securities (usually bonds) that are purchased and held until years later, when the bonds come due or the stocks are sold off. In effect, this is a custom-made index fund, particularly if it concentrates on blue-chip stocks. But because a custom-made UIT is likely to emphasize certain economic sectors and underweight others, it is somewhat more risky than the typical stock index fund.

Yet a stock UIT may be even more profitable than an index fund. One unit investment trust, Lexington Corporate Leaders (still open to new investors), has regularly outperformed Vanguard Index Trust 500, a fund modeled after the Standard & Poor's 500 Stock Index (see Chapter 9).

An investor could customize a UIT, using some of the 25 stocks (mostly blue chips) recommended by the 24 money managers interviewed for this book (see Chapter 16).

Almost as safe as a stock UIT of blue chips is a diversified portfolio of mutual funds. In a previous book of mine (*The Ultimate Mutual Fund*

Guide), various experts concluded that an investor should own five to eight different mutual funds. These funds should follow different tactics. One fund might concentrate on large companies, one on mid-sized, one on small. (Over the years, small companies apparently do better than mid-sized companies, which in turn do better than large companies.) The funds should also follow different tactics, the two major ones being buying what you hope are undervalued stocks and buying the stocks of fast-growing companies. (For more on the differences between the value and growth styles, see Chapter 3.)

Less safe is a portfolio of only a few mutual funds, or a portfolio of individual stocks managed by a professional, who might be a money manager or, indirectly, a newsletter. As mentioned, according to *The Hulbert Financial Digest*, among the best-performing newsletters over the last decade or so have been *The Value Line Investment Survey* (800-634-3583), the *Chartist* (310-596-2385), *BI Research* (P.O. Box 133, Redding, Conn. 06875), and *Zweig Forecast* (516-223-3800).

Still less safe: investments in sector funds. This strategy may not be common, but I have met people whose entire portfolios consist of various mutual funds that specialize in biotechnology, communications, or other narrow industries.

The riskiest portfolio is surely the hodge-podge that many people own and manage, or pretend to manage, by themselves. I have met many older investors whose portfolios consist of a baffling potpourri of stocks that various brokers had recommended over the years.

Here's how these various investment strategies might rank in terms of safety (defined as giving the investor a good chance of participating in stock market profits, without a strong possibility of exceptional and severe losses):

Safety Rankings of Stock Market Investment Strategies

Safest	A diversified stock index fund
Almost as safe	A fairly diversified unit investment trust of stocks
High safety	A diversified portfolio of actively managed, diversified mutual funds
Fairly safe to somewhat risky	Portfolio of a few actively managed, diversified mutual funds

Safety Rankings of Stock Market Investment Strategies (concluded)

	Portfolio actively managed by professionals (money manager, newsletter)
Risky	Nondiversified portfolio of sector or other nondiversified mutual funds
Very risky	Nondiversified portfolio, managed by nonprofessional investor

The next chapter will explain why almost all investors should own stocks—and why, along with all the roads to Jerusalem, there seem to be many roads to Sodom and Gomorrah as well.

Chapter 2

Stocks: Where the Big Money Is

By now, almost everyone must know that stocks are among the best investments for ordinary investors, being rivaled only by, perhaps, residential real estate.

From 1926 through 1994, common stocks (that is, the Standard & Poor's 500 Stock Index) rose 10 percent a year, according to data kept by Ibbotson Associates in Chicago. Five-year government notes went up 5 percent a year. Treasury bills (similar to money market funds and other short-term investments), 3.7 percent.

If you had invested $100 in stocks in 1926, it would have grown to $81,053.79. The same $100 in bonds would have grown to $3,084.33. And the same $100 would be worth only $1,218.62 if you had put the money into Treasury bills.

And when you consider that common stocks are less vulnerable to taxes—because much of their appreciation has come from capital gains, which have usually been taxed leniently—there's no contest. Stocks are where the big money is.

Yet many if not most investors manage to lose money in the stock market—or at least not to do as well as they should.

A few years ago, a Certified Financial Planner, Michael S. Gilbert of Clifton, New Jersey, checked the stock market portfolios of 250 of his clients to see how they had fared before consulting him. How many of their portfolios had outperformed fixed-income investments? Answer: three.

Eighty percent of the 250 investors owned five stocks or fewer, Gilbert reports.

His theory: These investors had bought on tips. (Tips, of course, can vary in their reliability. An offhand stock tip from your physician is different from a tip from *Money* magazine, or from a tip to buy shares of National Buggywhip Corporation from National Buggywhip's executive vice-president.) Or, after these investors had purchased stocks that turned out to be dogs, they anxiously waited and waited for them to rebound—instead of just selling them and moving on. (One of the telltale signs of novice investors is having trouble selling losers.)

But it isn't just beginners who manage to lose money in the stock market.

The notorious Steadman funds, run by Charles Steadman in Washington, D.C., demonstrate that it's possible to lose money in stocks regularly and consistently even if you invest for many years—and, like Mr. Steadman, are a graduate of the Harvard Law School.

The name "Steadman," of course, is as notorious among investors as "Antonio Salieri" is among composers and "Ralph Branca" among baseball players.

Here's how the various Steadman funds have fared, as of early 1995:

Fund	10-Year Annual Return
Steadman American Industry	–10.65% (104 out of 104 growth and income funds)
Steadman Associated	0.56% (102 out of 104 growth and income funds)
Steadman Investment	–4.02% (103 out of 104 growth and income funds)
Steadman Ocean Technology & Growth	–13.79% (11 out of 11 sector funds and 778 out of all 778 funds)

The Steadman portfolios were not diversified. (Currently, their assets have been frozen by the SEC because of various management improprieties.) Not long ago, Steadman Associated had more than 11 percent of its assets in one speculative stock, Interco. ("Better investments lie elsewhere"—*Value Line*, Sept. 1, 1989.)

The funds also move around like mad, switching from stocks to bonds to convertibles and back. The funds have also engaged in wacky trading tactics, such as something called the Bockler Investment Strategy, which calls for buying a put and a call option on a stock, along with the stock itself.

The sorry record of the Steadman funds demonstrates that bad investors may not learn from their mistakes. At the beginning of 1995, the Steadman funds had already lost 9 percent, while the stock market had risen over 10 percent.

TYPE ALPHA AND TYPE BETA INVESTORS

The chief reason so many investors don't succeed in the stock market is that the market, and individual stocks, are volatile. Market prices bounce up and down—although over the years they wind up higher and higher. Even the stocks of superb companies may bounce too far up; even the stocks of not-so-good companies may bounce too far down.

Obviously, if stock prices or market prices went up steadily year after year, the market would not be so treacherous. It is the volatility of prices in the stock market that proves the undoing of so many investors, especially beginners.

These beginners expect that stocks will resemble the investments they are accustomed to: passbook savings accounts, money market funds, certificates of deposit. Day after day, relentlessly, predictably, these investments make more money. They are simple, safe investments, and typically they are the investments that most people cut their teeth on, the way most people begin to appreciate classical music after first listening to Chopin.

It is a sharp, nasty transition to the world of stocks, and even of bonds, where sudden, cruel losses alternate (frequently) with sudden, sharp gains. The cold, numbing shock of experiencing a loss in a stock is something that most investors have probably suffered. A young man I know, studying for his Ph.D. in biochemistry at Princeton, bought a stock, watched in horror as its price sank into the pit, and ever since has invested in short-term CDs. A co-worker of mine bailed out of the stock market entirely after the crash of 1987—and still has not returned.

These are Type Alpha investors: risk-averse. Careful. Intolerant of volatility. They have not made the transition to Type Beta investors— accepting of risk, tolerant of volatility. When good stocks go down, a Type Beta investor becomes interested and may begin buying. When a stock he or she owns goes down, a Type Beta investor may buy *more* shares.

Alpha investors tend to have too few stocks, and certainly not enough in different industries. I have heard veteran stockbrokers tell audiences that all an investor may need is a half-dozen stocks. (The evidence from academia is that you should have 20 stocks or so as a minimum, so as not to badly underperform the market. See Chapter 4).

Type Alpha investors, still inhabiting the world of passbook savings accounts and CDs, tend to be greedy for yield. Only infrequently may they have experienced the joy of receiving capital gains. Inquiring as to the yield of an investment is, to them, tantamount to kicking the tires. They are easily sold junk bonds and junky stocks. They haven't learned that high yields are warning signs: a high-yielding bond is likely to be a junk (low-rated) bond; a high-yielding stock is likely to be from a company in such hot water that it may be forced to cut or eliminate its dividend.

Alpha investors may also seek out stocks with low prices. To them, low prices are bargains. And, of course, they can be. You can buy large shares of penny stocks for very little money. (As a matter of fact, there's actually some evidence that low-priced stocks do unusually well, but the chief reason seems to be that low-priced stocks tend to be those of small companies, which apparently do best over time.) Besides, a lot of Type Alpha investors are on the prowl for low-priced stocks, and this helps drive up the prices. Another reason Alphas wind up with low-priced stocks is that the telemarketers pitch cheap stocks—not Exxon and Ameritech.

Type Alpha investors are also trusting and naive, at least to the extent of thinking that all stockbrokers, along with people they have never met except over the telephone, can give valuable guidance.

Once they begin investing in stocks, Type Alpha people tend to extrapolate. The number that comes after 1, 3, 5, and 7 is always 9. If a stock has been rising by leaps and bounds, you should buy it because it will continue rising. That's the way things usually work in the world—and even, sometimes, in the stock market. Extrapolation— generalizing from past performance—is wonderfully useful in life. Someone who is honest today can be relied on to be honest tomorrow; the author of a good novel, the director of a fine film, the composer of a catchy tune, can be expected to write another good novel, direct another fine film, compose another catchy tune. A baseball player who has hit .350 all year is the person you want hitting in a clutch situation, not a .200 hitter. If Donald Yacktman does well managing Selected

American Shares, he will do well managing a new fund, the Yacktman fund.

But when stock prices go up and up, they may become too expensive, and plummet. And stocks that go down and down may become underpriced. Type Beta investors know this; Type Alpha investors are still learning. They eat Boston Chicken and drink Snapple Beverage. They avoid whatever stocks are lingering in the dungeon, poised to rebound.

As mentioned, Type Alphas also may have trouble selling their losers. In the face of bad news, they become a little depressed and passive. Or they are assured by their stockbrokers that their stocks will rebound—which they very well may, sooner or later; very likely later. Ask veteran investors what advice to give to beginners, and they stress: Be patient. Good advice—if you are talking about stocks in general, or about any stock about which you know a great deal, but not the typically erratic stock that Alphas invest in.

No doubt the self-esteem of Alphas is also on the line. Selling a stock is an admission of an error—to oneself, to one's stockbroker, to the world.

And then there is the comforting notion that a loss is not a loss until the security is sold; only then is the loss "locked in." It is, in the cliché, a distinction without much difference.

Type Beta investors are no doubt readier to unload their losers. They may do it, in part, just to "clear their heads," as Michael Price of the Mutual Series funds once told me. Or because they have apparently decided that other investors know something they don't know, which is why those other investors are selling. Or because they recognize that they did make a mistake, or that something unpredictable and unfortunate happened (for example, a new product proved a disaster). Many Type Beta investors will sell their losers, for the tax loss, then— if they have confidence in the stock, or the industry—buy the same stock after waiting 31 days. (They delay so as not to run afoul of the wash sale rule, which prohibits deducting losses on securities you have sold if you buy them back fairly quickly.) Or they buy a similar stock immediately.

Beta investors may also hold onto their losers because they are convinced that they will rebound, not because their self-esteem is on the line. If unsure, they may loosen that hold.

Type Alpha investors tend to hold onto their losers—and to sell their

winners too soon. While superb investors may also sell too soon —
Bernard Baruch admitted that he always sold early — Alpha investors,
I suspect, sell far too soon. Perhaps they are so unaccustomed to
making a profit that they want to lock in their gains. Years ago, a writer
for *Forbes* magazine presented studies of average investors, showing
that they kept their losers and sold their winners. While the writer, as
it turned out, had used fictitious data, his premise supported what all
of us had suspected.

Beta investors may also sell too soon, as mentioned, but some of
them hedge their bets, taking only a few chips off the table.

The basic reason why Type Alpha investors hold onto their losers
too long and sell their winners too soon is clear: They aren't especially
knowledgable about the stocks that they have purchased. They don't
know whether a company's earnings have been growing and may
continue growing. Unlike analysts, they haven't spoken with the
company's officers or with the company's competitors and suppliers.
They probably don't read the professional journals that cover the area.
They don't know what sophisticated investors are saying and doing.
They are just plain uninformed, both as to qualitative and quantitative
information. They buy stocks on tips because they simply don't know
what else to do.

Alphas also don't have a strategy, a plan. They buy this and that,
whereas professional investors tend to specialize in certain stocks,
about which they become expert. If you spend years searching for
undervalued stocks, for example, you are more likely to be able to
detect the sometimes subtle differences between truly undervalued
stocks and stocks that amply deserve their seemingly low prices.

Type Alpha investors, furthermore, probably aren't sure how their
investments have fared. I attended a meeting where Arthur Levitt Jr.,
the chairman of the Securities and Exchange Commission, asked the
audience how many of them knew—really knew—how their
investments had performed the previous year. Perhaps 5 percent did.
Not surprising. If you buy and sell frequently, and reinvest your
dividends, it's hard to keep track of your gains and losses. Also, many
Alpha investors probably don't know enough to compare their
portfolio's performance to an appropriate index like the Standard &
Poor's 500 or a balanced-fund index. And brokerage reports don't help
you out. (It's easier to calculate your performance, of course, if you
don't trade very often, and if you invest mainly in mutual funds.)

If you know that your investments have performed poorly, you may be impelled to discover the reason why and to change your tactics. (I suspect that most people invest in individual stocks in their 20s and 30s, then move over into mutual funds in their 40s when they have finally seen the light.)

Alpha investors also may be guided by stockbrokers, who typically recommend individual stocks and suggest that shareholders trade them fairly frequently. Recommending blue-chip stocks and urging investors to hold on to them is not the way stockbrokers make commissions.

These unfortunate investors are also guided by their emotions. They hold onto a stock because a beloved relative bequeathed it to them, or because they once worked (or still work) for the company. Or because the stock did well once, and they would feel ungrateful if they parted with it. Or they avoid liquor companies, tobacco companies, companies that make *racy* movies, and so forth.

I myself am holding onto my AT&T in part because, years ago, my son entered a mathematics project in a science contest and was one of the winners. But the contest's sponsors had provided awards only for students submitting science projects, not math projects. At the last minute AT&T came up with an award for math projects—a calculator. God bless you, AT&T.

Type Alpha investors, let us not forget, are our brothers, or ourselves as we were years ago. And let us not forget that there are few pure Alpha investors, few pure Beta investors.

Here is a summary of some of the reasons Type Alpha investors don't make money in the stock market, in approximate order of importance:

- They don't own enough stocks, in different industries.
- They don't have good information about their stocks, don't know where to get such information, and might not know to interpret the information:
- They buy high-priced stocks and avoid low-priced stocks.
- They buy on tips.
- After experiencing any loss, they panic, and either sell too soon or hold the stock too long.
- They sell their winners too soon.

- They don't specialize in certain types of stocks and stock strategies.
- They don't know how poorly their investments have done.
- They are trusting and naive, and rely too much on stockbrokers and telemarketers.
- They are too much interested in yields.
- In buying and selling, they may be guided by irrelevant sentiment.

Chapter 3

The Value versus Growth Styles

Value investors are like baseball teams that buy ballplayers in a prolonged slump, players with sore arms or injured knees, or those approaching their 40s and seemingly washed up. Such ballplayers come relatively cheap.

Growth investors are like baseball teams that buy young, vigorous .300 hitters and 20-game winners. These players are expensive, but perhaps worth it if they continue hitting .300 and winning 20 games for several more seasons. Considering how expensive they are, though, it's a risky business. Stocks with high price/earnings ratios, once they take a hit, go down fast and furiously.

A Nobel Laureate, William F. Sharpe, has found that the value/ growth distinction—along with the size of the companies that money managers buy—explains some 90 percent of the differences between the returns of stock mutual funds.

It is one of the few basic principles of stock market investing that stocks tend to become excessively high priced or excessively low priced because investors tend to go to extremes, both in selling and buying. Even professional investors may contribute to the polarity, buying high-flying stocks just to have them appear in the portfolio at the end of a quarter, when their portfolio is to be opened to public scrutiny. And they may sell losers for the same reason, thus driving down their prices still further.

VALUE STOCKS

The value strategy calls for buying stocks of companies under a cloud. Perhaps their earnings have faltered, the dividend is being cut, lawsuits are impending, the officers have made seemingly improvident decisions (to buy another company, for example, for too high a price), there is internal dissension, or key corporate leaders are leaving. Whatever the reason, the stock is unwanted and unloved.

The stigmata of a value stock are mainly:

1. A low price/earnings ratio (compared to the company's usual ratio, compared to the ratio of similar companies, compared to the stock market as a whole). The price/earnings ratio indicates how fond of a stock investors are. The stocks of growing companies tend to have high p/e ratios, or multiples. The stocks of stodgy companies—blue chips, utilities—tend to have low p/e ratios.

2. Low price-to-book ratios. Book value is what the company would actually be worth, per share, if it were sold off. A book value of 3 or more is considered high; a book value below 1 is considered attractive. But the calculation of book value has been criticized of late because of the flexibility that the calculators of price-book ratios enjoy.

3. A higher than normal dividend yield. This is the result of lowering the price/earnings ratio, assuming that the company was paying out a normal dividend before the price sank. (A company in such trouble that eliminates its dividend, of course, may be a value stock, too.)

4. Less volatility.

5. Relatively greater gains from income than from price appreciation.

Many value stocks are cyclical and industrial companies (autos, manufacturing, steel, basic materials), which benefit from economic expansion and suffer from economic declines.

Value investors are betting on change. They think a ballplayer's sore arm will heal, that a company will recover. Their philosophy is that ugly ducklings may grow into beautiful swans.

Contrarianism is a variant of the value strategy. You do the opposite of what other investors are doing. It is a broader style than the value style: It could lead not just to buying unwanted stocks, but to the selling short of stocks of companies that are too unwisely loved. (You sell short as a way of betting that a stock's price will go down.) A contrarian is also more likely to practice market timing, going against the majority of other investors when they are optimistic or pessimistic.

The chief pitfall of the value strategy is that you may buy dogs that aren't just temporarily masquerading as dogs, but dogs that are really and truly and permanently dogs. Although the value strategy assumes that ugly ducklings will grow into beautiful swans, most of the time ugly ducklings grow into ugly ducks. One famous contrarian investor bought the shares of an ailing airline a few hours before the airline declared bankruptcy.

A key difference between successful and unsuccessful value managers may lie in their ability to distinguish truly undervalued stocks from stocks that deserve their low prices. This may be a function of more information, or better insight. Some value managers claim that they don't buy a seemingly undervalued stock unless they see a "catalyst"—a reason why the stock should revive, such as new management with new ideas.

GROWTH STOCKS

Growth stocks include many food, drug, tobacco, beverage, and health care companies, which tend to lag during periods of economic growth.

The chief stigmata of growth stocks are:

1. Relatively high price-book ratios.
2. High returns on equity.
3. Above-average gains in sales and earnings (10 percent–15 percent annually or more).
4. Higher price/earnings multiples than value stocks (ideally, the p/e ratio is not above the annual earnings/growth rate).
5. Few or no dividends.
6. Greater volatility.
7. Relatively greater income from capital gains.

Growth or momentum stocks are those of companies whose earnings have been growing steadily. Some managers look for companies with growth over a certain period, say, three or five years; others look for a specific level of growth, say 10 percent or 20 percent a year; still others look for companies of a certain size with a certain, regular growth pattern.

The challenge is to find such companies early, before their price shoots up; and to sell them early, before their prices go too high—which is what tends to happen to high-flying stocks.

Another challenge is to determine how healthy a rise in earnings is. For example, earnings may rise because of cost-cutting—employees are let go, for example. An investor might have more confidence in a company if the earnings were rising simply because of increased sales.

A variant on growth investing is the rising-dividend strategy, which seems to have been invented by William Lippman, who runs Franklin Rising Dividend and introduced the Pilgrim MagnaCap Fund. Obviously, a company that regularly raises its dividends is probably enjoying healthy growth.

Other ways of gauging rising earnings would be to look at rising sales, or cash flow, or return on equity, all of which might provide different kinds of clues as to how sustainable the earnings increase is. The more clues, the better.

Whereas value investors count on change, growth investors bet on inertia, that objects in motion will remain in motion, that companies with good earnings will continue enjoying good earnings. They hope that trees grow to the sky—but they are prepared to sell when the trees' growth slows.

As Warren Buffett has said, the growth and the value styles are joined at the hip. Value stocks can become growth stocks, and vice versa. A growing company's earnings may falter, thanks to competition. Its price may fall so far that it becomes a value stock. Once the company recovers, it may become a growth stock again. That's what happened to IBM not too long ago. A growth investor would have bought it while it was growing and sold it when it began faltering. A value investor would have purchased it on the way down, or on the way back up.

Many investors do not stay exclusively in either the growth or value camps. Some growth investors buy "growth at a price" (GAAP). They might be classified as growth/value investors. Some value investors want to see some growth, some sign of recovery, before they hop on board. These people might be classified as value/growth investors.

In between, of course, are the blend investors, who buy both growth and value stocks, or everything. (Growth-and-income mutual funds tend to be targeted toward investors who want growth stocks along with value stocks.)

The typical index fund is a blend of value and growth, but a passive blend. An active blend would mean that the manager bought undervalued stocks along with growth stocks—or bought stocks in the blurred middle.

So, all in all, there's a continuum: GROWTH . . . growth/ value . . . blend . . . value/growth . . . VALUE

Why don't all growth investors perform alike, and all value investors?

The outcomes depend to a large extent on the size of the companies they buy. For one thing, research is probably more important if you buy small-company stocks because less is known about them. And if you concentrate on larger companies, you can be a more active manager, selling and buying more frequently without affecting the market.

Besides, few managers are pure. Most value managers buy some growth stocks, and vice versa.

There are other reasons why growth and value managers may have different results. They may buy or sell earlier or later; they may gravitate toward certain sectors of the economy; they may use different statistical measures of growth: How many years in a row should the earnings have increased? By what amount? Or they may use different statistical measures of value: How far down should the price/earnings ratio or price-book ratio have fallen? Should you wait for some sign or symptom of recovery?

Another important dimension: Do the managers stress quantitative or qualitative evidence? Some managers primarily look at computer screens: growth rate, price-book ratio, return on equity, and so forth. Others also interview management, and check whether management owns shares, whether the company is buying back its own shares, and what competitors and suppliers say about the company.

Quantitative investors probably tend to be growth investors, while qualitative investors tend to be value investors. Numbers probably have more influence on short-term performance, which is what growth investors are especially interested in, and less influence on longer-term performance.

These are broad generalizations. Some value managers pay attention almost exclusively to statistics—for example, stocks with higher-than-average yields. Some growth managers do extensive person-to-person research. The Janus family and the Strong family are famous for going out into the field.

Investors who specialize in smaller companies are typically growth managers, unless they buy companies that were once larger but— owing to hard times—now have lower capitalizations. There aren't many small-company value investors.

The growth style and the value style take turns at center stage. One theory is that, as the economy slows down, people run toward companies whose earnings remain brisk. Whereas when the economy picks up, growth stocks become just one among many—and value stocks start rebounding. But Gregory McCrickard, a T. Rowe Price fund manager, believes that "There's no formula that tells you when the market focus will shift from growth to value or vice versa."

Further clues to the differences between the value style and the growth style come from a value stock-market index and a growth stock-market index, created in 1992 by Standard & Poor's Corporation and BARRA, an investment technology firm in Berkeley, California.

The two indexes are divided according to one simple marker: price-book ratios. Value stocks have the lower price-book ratios; growth stocks have the higher ratios. The indexes are rebalanced on January 1 and July 1 every year. The turnover between value and growth stocks has averaged about 20 percent a year—not high, considering that many stocks originally assigned to each of the categories were borderline.

Here are important statistics for the two indexes as of June 30, 1992:

Characteristic	Value	Growth
Number of companies	322	178
Weighted average capitalization	$16,716 mil.	$25,804 mil.
Median capitalization	$ 2,272	$3,616
Price/earnings ratio	27.44	22.65
IBES predicted p/e ratio	12.76	15.96
Price-book ratio	1.51	4.21

Characteristic	Value	Growth
Indicated dividend yield	3.85	2.25
Return on equity	6.90	24.22
BARRA predicted beta*	0.94	1.06

*Beta is a measure of volatility.

Why are growth companies likely to be bigger? Because the largest companies tend to be growing companies, like Coca-Cola, General Electric, AT&T, and Philip Morris. That's why they remain so large. (It's because growth companies are so large that fewer companies are in the growth index: The two indexes are intended to have similar total market capitalizations.) Small, developing companies also tend to be growth, as mentioned, whereas mid-caps to large-caps tend to be value.

Value stocks, as expected, have far lower price-book ratios; lower predicted price/earnings ratios as measured by IBES, a company that tracks analysts' predictions; higher dividend yields; lower return on equity; and lower volatility.

Surprisingly, price/earnings ratios for growth stocks were lower, the reason being that in 1992 several very large companies in the value index, like General Motors, suffered big losses. With lower earnings, their price/earnings ratios shot way up.

The value index was heavily concentrated in energy, utility, and financial sectors. That helps explain the lower volatility of value stocks—along with the fact that the prices of value stocks are rather low already.

When the S&P/BARRA value and growth indexes were tracked back to 1975, an interesting discovery was made: Value stocks had done much better, with lower volatility to boot. The annualized return of the value index from January 1975 through June 1992 was 16.97 percent. The return of the growth index was 13.86 percent. The beta of the value index was 0.92; the beta of the growth index, 1.07.

If there must be a reason, George Sauter—who runs Vanguard's real-world value and growth index funds—has given one: Owners of value stocks pay more in the taxes, because such stocks bless you with more in the way of taxable dividends. So once you pay taxes, value stocks may do only as well as growth stocks. Here I think we are in the realm of Rudyard Kipling's "Just So" stories. There doesn't have to be a rational explanation why value stocks, during a certain time period, have outperformed growth stocks. Maybe they shouldn't have. It could have been an aberration. Someone has pointed out that the 1970s were a good decade for value stocks, so the starting point of the race may have determined the outcome.

In any case, John Rekenthaler, editor of Morningstar's *5-Star Investor*, reports that growth mutual funds have handily outperformed value mutual funds, at least as far back as 1980.

Very likely, there is a greater distance between the best and worst growth investors than the best and worst value investors. One reason: There's more volatility in growth stocks. So, if someone is investing in a growth-style mutual fund, he or she might give it less leeway before selling than that person should give to a value-style mutual fund.

Not surprisingly, by and large our own panelists tended to vote for either value stocks or growth stocks as the better performer, depending on their own particular philosophy.

Here are their answers to the question, do growth or value stocks do better in the long run? (In parentheses are the panelists' strategies.)

Art Bonnel: growth (growth)
Rudy Carryl: growth (growth)
Robert Christensen: value (value)
James Craig: growth (growth)
Maureen Cullinane: growth (growth)
Hugh Denison: value (value)
Richard Fentin: equal (value)
Mario Gabelli: equal (value)
Peter Hagerman: equal (blend)
Richard Huson: value (value)
Warren Isabelle: equal (value)
Arnold Kaufman: NA (blend)
Warren Lammert: NA (blend)
William Lippman/Bruce Baughman: "Neither. Good selection does better." (value)
Thomas Marsico: growth (growth)
Terry Milberger: growth (blend)
Gary Pilgrim: growth (growth)

Michael Price: value (value)

Douglas Ramos: value (value)

Brian Rogers: value (value)

Eileen Rominger: value—"The way I define value." (value)

Robert Sanborn: value (value)

Peter Schliemann: value (value)

Ralph Seger: growth—"Growth must be combined with value. By value, I mean the current p/e ratio, based on estimated earnings per share 12 months out, must be less than the historic average p/e ratio." (growth)

Sandra Shrewsbury: growth (growth)

Richard Strong: growth (growth)

Heiko Thieme: growth (growth)

Peter Van Dyke: growth (growth)

Donald Yacktman: "Buy good businesses at low valuations." (blend)

A famous value investor is Michael Price, who runs the Mutual Series funds in Short Hills, N.J. He is also one of this book's panelists. In its September 30, 1994, issue, Morningstar reported that Mutual Shares owned 193 stocks. Their average price/earnings ratio, 18.4, was 91 percent of the S&P 500's average p/e ratio. Their price-book ratio was 2.6, or 0.74 percent of the S&P 500. Their five-year earnings growth was 8.6 percent, or 54 percent more than the S&P 500. Their return on assets was 5.5 percent, only 0.76 percent of the S&P. Debt as a percentage of total capitalization was 30.7 percent, 1.05 percent more than the S&P.

The fund's expense ratio for 1993 was 0.74. Its standard deviation (a measure of volatility) was 7.2, its beta (another measure of volatility) a little more than half of that of the S&P 500.

The yield of Mutual Shares was 3.5 percent. In 1993, its capital gains were over four times its income (the total return was 21.0 percent). Its turnover rate was a mere 49 percent (a rate of 100 percent suggests that the entire portfolio turned over). Mutual Series was invested about one-third in financial stocks, almost three times their representation in the S&P 500.

Why was the fund's earnings growth rate higher than the S&P, considering that it follows the value strategy? Probably because the stocks it buys are smaller than S&P stocks: Mutual Shares is considered a mid-cap fund, buying stocks with an average capitalization (price times shares outstanding) of $2.481 billion, only 18 percent of the Standard & Poor's 500's average stock.

James Craig, a famous growth stock investor, runs the Janus Fund. He also served as a panelist for this book. Janus's statistics, compared with those of Mutual Shares, are below:

	Mutual Shares	Janus
Price/earnings ratio	18.4	23.2
Price-book ratio	2.6	4.0
5-year earnings growth	8.6	10.7
Return on assets	5.5%	6.2%
Debt as % total cap	30.7%	28.8%
Expense ratio	0.74 (1993)	0.92% (1993)
Standard deviation	7.2	9.87
Beta	0.53	0.93
Yield	3.5%	1.9%
Gains divided by income	2.4 (1993)	4.2 (1993)
Turnover rate	49% (1993)	127% (1993)
Heaviest sector	Financials	Consumer durables

Janus's expenses were higher. Is this generally true of growth funds? Possibly—because of the higher turnover, greater research is needed to track new stocks.

Growth companies also seem to be in better shape financially, having less debt compared with their total capitalization, and enjoying a higher return on assets.

On turnovers, growth funds in general averaged 97.8 percent, while value funds averaged 83.4 percent.

George Sauter believes that, in fact, value funds have lower turnovers "because it takes a while before they turn around." Value stocks, he goes on, will tend to form a saucer-shaped bottom of a curve. When their prices reach their low, they tend to remain there for a few years before climbing up. Growth stocks bounce back faster.

Sauter also thinks that a value investor will hold a stock twice as long as a growth investor, who sells a stock as soon as the company's fortunes begin fading.

Are value investors likely to own more stocks in their portfolios, so a few winners are subsidizing the losers? Sauter thinks so. And, as we'll see in Chapter 4, value investors in our panel recommended that individual investors have 15 to 20 stocks, whereas growth investors recommended 10 to 15 stocks.

What about diversification? Janus had an R squared (a measure of how the performance of a fund tracks the S&P 500) of 87 recently. Vanguard/Windsor II, a similarly large *value* fund that also invests in large companies, had a recent R squared of 90. So it may be that the amount of diversification isn't linked with the value or growth tactics but the preferences of the fund manager.

The statistics of Mutual Shares are close to those of Vanguard Index Value Fund, just as Janus's statistics are close to those of Vanguard's Growth Index Fund. (Exception: The return on assets of Janus's average holding is surprisingly low.)

The sectors that Vanguard Value was heaviest in, during late 1994, were energy, utilities, financials, and consumer durables. It held relatively few health stocks. Of its holdings, 20.8 percent were in utilities, 1.7 percent in health.

Mutual Shares, by contrast, was heavy in health, light in utilities and energy. The fund had only 4.5 percent of its portfolio in utilities, but 9.0 percent in health. It's clear, now, why two value investors may have different results: They may emphasize different sectors.

Here is a comparision of various statistics for the Standard & Poor's 500 Index, Vanguard Value Index, and Vanguard Index growth. (The expense ratios are all nearly identical, but may not reflect the real world because Vanguard runs the funds the same way.)

	S&P 500*	Value Index**	Growth Index**
Price/earnings ratio	20.1	18.0 (0.89)	22.8 (1.11)
Price-book ratio	3.5	2.1 (0.59)	4.8 (1.39)
5-yr earnings growth	5.6	0.4 (0.07)	10.4 (1.91)
Return on assets	7.3	4.2 (0.57)	9.7 (1.45)
Debt % total cap	29.1%	33.0%	25.4%
Expense ratio	0.19%	.20%	.20%
Standard deviation	10.02%	na	na
Beta	1.00	na	na

	S&P 500*	Value Index**	Growth Index**
Yield	2.5%	3.1%	2.1%
Turnover rate	6%	30%	36%
Heaviest sector:	industrial cylicals	energy	health

*The figures are for Vanguard Index Trust 500, a replica of the S&P 500.

**Numbers in parentheses compare the numbers with the S&P 500.

Source: Morningstar.

Other possible differences between the value and growth strategies relate to the personalities of their managers.

Apparently value managers must be patient, self-confident, Type B people (calm, noncompetitive, not prone to heart attacks). The hobby of the former manager of Vanguard/Windsor, John Neff, I have been told, is collecting fine wines—and waiting for them to mature. A suitable metaphor.

Sauter thinks that instinct is an important attribute of value investors: They must buy a stock when "the market is selling that stock ruthlessly." And whereas value managers tend to be contrarians, growth managers tend to be "the exact opposite: They are typically buying what's been hot recently, what's on a real roll."

Growth managers apparently must also be opportunistic, flexible, Type A people (competitive, ambitious, emotional, prone to heart attacks). They must be ready to move on a dime, to buy and especially to sell.

Sauter claims that "growth investors tend to have more personal biases. They will have their own pet loves and hates" among areas to invest in.

Of course, Type A people can probably turn into Type B people, and vice versa, depending on what tasks they are assigned.

Just as growth stocks may turn into value stocks, and value stocks become growth stocks, investors themselves may be classified as one or the other, depending on their current styles.

Morningstar classifed the American Heritage Fund—run by Heiko Thieme, one of our panelists—as a mid-sized blend fund in 1991, as a small-company growth fund in 1992, as a small-company value fund in 1993, and again as a small-company growth fund in 1994. Not surprising, considering that Thieme's fund may own small-company stocks (like Spectrum Information Technology) as well as IBM, Philip Morris, Merck, Eastman Kodak, and UAL.

It isn't always easy to identify growth investors and value investors. Some growth investors, I'm told, claim to be value investors only because it's considered a more conservative approach, and therefore more attractive to most current and future clients.

Other investors claim to be either value or growth, depending on what style has been ascendant lately.

In general, it may be better for investors to choose the general strategy, value or growth, more appropriate to their personalities, than to try to be ambidextrous.

Other investment strategies exist. Market timers bet that entire markets will go up or down, perhaps based on the season of the year. There's also the momentum style: Buying stocks that are rising, selling those that are falling.

Nevertheless, the three strategies described above—value, growth, and blend—are the pre-eminent.

Chapter 4

The Dow Dividend Strategy

The Dow Dividend Strategy is a seemingly surefire way to make money in the stock market. It is actually a variant of the value strategy, buying undervalued stocks. You buy 5 or 10 of the highest-yielding stocks among the 30 in the Dow Jones Industrial Average. (You could also buy just the single highest-yielding stock.) Those stocks have high yields because their prices are relatively low. At the end of a year, you sell those stocks, moving over to a new top-5 or top-10 list of highest-yielding stocks (assuming that the list has changed).

This tactic supposedly guarantees that, over the years, you will outperform the entire Dow.

The May 1994 issue of the *Journal of the American Association of Individual Investors* featured an article titled "The Dow Dividend Strategy: How It Works—and Why." And if that dense, tightly packed article didn't answer all of your questions, you could have read a piece in *Forbes* magazine (May 23, 1994) that explained why the Dow Dividend Strategy *doesn't* work ("High Yield, High Risk").

The AAII article, by three academics, noted that the strategy has been shown to hold true for the years 1957 through 1991. Various brokers have even set up unit investment trusts employing the strategy. (*Fortune* magazine has argued that it's cheaper just to buy the stocks directly). There's even a newsletter on the subject.

The academics themselves found that from January 1973 through December 1992 the ever-changing top-yielding stocks had an annualized total return of 16.06 percent, versus only 10.91 percent for the 30 Dow stocks. (Transaction costs weren't included.) They suspect that the strategy works because stocks move to extremes of overvaluation and undervaluation, and any extreme in one direction will be followed by an opposite extreme. In other words, they roundly endorse the inefficient market theory—the notion that stocks are not always reasonably priced.

To test this theory, they checked how the 10 highest-yielding stocks every year from 1957 to 1991 had performed in the year before they were chosen. Yes, indeed, they had underperformed the market (by 5.99 percent)—and were poised to turn from ugly ducklings into swans. The 20 remaining lower-yielding stocks, naturally, had outperformed the market (by 3.18 percent).

The strategy, by the way, seems to work best if you start in January, thanks to the "January effect"—stocks, especially small-company stocks, tend to do very well in the first month of the year. Trying to start in December, to beat the crowd, may not work because the Dow dogs become especially flea-bitten in December, thanks to tax selling.

Probably the strategy works because the 10 highest-yielding Dow stocks have lower price/earnings ratios and are generally undervalued. Thirty-odd studies have confirmed that low p/e stocks do better than other stocks. A lower p/e, in other words, is the chief clue to identifying ugly ducklings that may be swans in disguise.

Mark Hulbert, who monitors newsletter performance, dismissed the Dow Dividend Strategy in *Forbes* magazine. But what he mainly objected to was only an extreme version of the strategy, using only a single stock. Studies have shown that this version is the most risky, but can also be the most rewarding. In 1994, the highest-yielding stock at the beginning of the year was Woolworth, which proceeded to lose one-third of its value.

Hulbert scores some points. A danger with high-yielding stocks, he notes, is that dividends may be reduced. In fact, that may be why the yields are so high in the first place: Investors doubt that such yields can be maintained. So you've got to look for a stock with a strong balance sheet, too.

Besides, Hulbert argues, a high yield may not even be a unerring sign that a stock is overvalued: The yield may be high compared with other (Dow) stocks, but not compared with its own usual yield. (A counterargument is that the actual yield doesn't matter; what matters, in view of changing competitive interest rates, is relative yield.)

The lessons seem to be that no mechanistic stock market strategy is totally reliable, and that human intervention can be useful.

Still, it is well to remember that the Dow Dividend Strategy, from 1973 through 1992, did manage to beat the Dow with 10 stocks—even though the Dow itself did better in 5 of those 20 years.

Chapter 5

Meet the Panelists

Here are brief biographies of the panelists who responded to the questionnaire about their investing strategies:

Arthur J. Bonnel, Manager

ACCOLADE BONNEL GROWTH FUND, RENO

Assets under management: $14 million

Years of investment experience: 20

Strategy: "Strong earnings, low debt. Good balance sheet and management ownership. I would attribute my success to my experience as a floor trader. I understand how and why markets work, then I follow my system."

Biography: Born in 1945, Bonnel is a graduate of the University of Nevada, with a B.A. in economics and an MBA. He spent 14 years as president of his own investment advisory firm, which he founded in 1973. Bonnel managed MIM Stock Appreciation from 1987 until March 1994. In 1993, *Fortune* magazine called him the best growth-fund manager in America. In 1994 he started his own mutual fund under the aegis of the United Services Fund of San Antonio.

Rudy Carryl, Director

MACKAY-SHIELDS FINANCIAL CORP., NEW YORK CITY

Assets under management: $11.5 billion

Years of investment experience: 5

Strategy: "Disciplined, bottom-up stock selection approach."

Biography: Born in 1951 in Guyana, South America, Carryl obtained a B.A. in geology from the University of London. He spent 14 years with Value Line as research director and senior portfolio manager before joining MacKay-Shields in 1992.

Robert A. Christensen

SENIOR VICE-PRESIDENT AND PORTFOLIO MANAGER

STEIN ROE & FARNHAM, CHICAGO

Assets under management: $750 million

Years of investment experience: 32

Strategy: "Low price-earnings ratio strategy, with diversification similar to S&P 500."

Biography: Christensen obtained a B.A. from Vanderbilt University in 1955 and an MBA from Harvard in 1962. He has been with Stein Roe since then. He is a Chartered Investment Counselor.

James P. Craig

VICE PRESIDENT AND PORTFOLIO MANAGER

THE JANUS FUND (HE ALSO SERVES AS PORTFOLIO MANAGER OF THE JANUS BALANCED FUND AND BOTH THE JANUS ASPEN SERIES GROWTH AND BALANCED PORTFOLIOS.)

Assets under management: $11.7 billion

Years of investment experience (at Janus): 12

Strategy: "We add value through analysis of future earnings. Simply, we get paid when we more accurately predict earnings than the rest of the street. That is our added value, or edge. Strict adherence to this discipline and avoiding 'leads' and panic spells gives us superior long-term performance."

Biography: Prior to Janus, Craig served as an investment analyst with Trust Company of the West. After graduating from the University of Alabama with an undergraduate degree in business, he received his master's in finance and was a teaching assistant in finance at the Wharton School, University of Pennsylvania. He joined Janus Capital Corporation in May 1993.

Maureen E. Cullinane

VICE PRESIDENT AND SENIOR PORTFOLIO MANAGER

KEYSTONE CUSTODIAN FUNDS, BOSTON

Assets under management: $350 million

Years of investment experience: 20

Strategy: "In general, we look for companies with earnings growth better than the S&P 500. We particularly want to select those companies whose earnings growth is actually accelerating; for example, a company whose earnings have been growing at a 15 percent rate may now have an earnings growth of 20 percent because of a new product, technology, or corporate restructuring. In general, stocks appreciate when earnings growth accelerates.

"We also like to concentrate our investments; we try to limit the number of stocks held in the portfolio to about 50, so that we can maximize the impact of an investment.

"Finally, we have a selling discipline. When we buy a stock, we set a target price, where we think the stock will be selling the next year. Our target price is based on our earnings estimate, the relative price/earnings ratio of the stock. As the target price approaches, we reassess the fundamentals. If the stock appears fairly valued, we will sell the stock. We may also be wrong in our estimates of earnings growth. We will sell a stock whenever there is a decline in earnings."

Biography: After obtaining an M.A. in French from Emmanuel College in 1970 , Cullinane joined Keystone in 1974. She received an M.B.A. in finance from Boston University in 1981, and a Chartered Financial Analyst designation in 1984.

Hugh F. Denison

DIRECTOR OF RESEARCH

HEARTLAND ADVISORS

Assets under management: $700 million

Years of investment experience: 25

Strategy: Our disciplined investment approach employs 10 "value" parameters for research, evaluation, stock selection, and ongoing portfolio review.

1. LOW PRICE/EARNINGS MULTIPLE.

A stock's price/earnings multiple should be less than the market's general multiple. Furthermore, the earnings yield should be greater than the rate available on AAA long-term corporate bonds. This provides the opportunity for multiple expansion and prevents the purchase of stock that could have considerable risk if earnings contract.

2. HIGH CASH FLOW.

Cash flow per share should be considerably higher than earnings per share. A strong cash flow allows a company to generate wealth over the long term. Debt does not need to be added as quickly, if at all, for expansion or reinvestment. A high discretionary cash flow, after capital expenditure and dividends, is very attractive.

3. THE COMPANY SHOULD BE EXHIBITING INCREASED EARNINGS GROWTH.

Also, the consistency and quality of earnings, based on conservative accounting practices, is an important factor.

4. DISCOUNT TO BOOK VALUE.

The stock should be selling below its tangible book value per share. (Tangible book value is equal to total assets minus all liabilities and good will.) Changes in earnings and price/earnings ratios can be sudden and violent. Changes in book value are more gradual.

5. FINANCIAL SOUNDNESS.

Long-term debt should be generally less than 25 percent of total capitalization. During difficult periods, a company's cash flow should be directed to investments in operations rather than interest expense. A highly leveraged balance sheet can become a hindrance to performance and endanger the company's very existence. High liquidity is also important. The company's current assets less current liabilities and long-term debt, per share, should be high in relation to the price of the stock.

6. INSIDER OWNERSHIP.

Ownership of stock by insiders rather than institutions indicates that management and directors have their personal wealth invested in the company and its performance. Additionally, the company should be run by capable and honest management with a history of reasonable and fair relations with shareholders.

7. DIVIDEND STABILITY.

The dividend must not have been cut more than once in the last 10 years. Dividends that are consistent and that increase regularly are given preference in weighting. Dividend stability demonstrates management's ability to handle cash flow and earnings for the benefit of shareholders.

8. HIDDEN ASSETS.

Assets that are not on the balance sheet or that have appreciated above their book value increase their stock's underlying worth. Hidden assets such as LIFO reserve [money set aside for sales taxed on a "last-in, first-out" basis], understated natural resources, or fixed assets worth substantially more than their book values can significantly add to the stock's net worth.

9. CHART PATTERN.

Technical analysis should indicate that a stock is presently attractive for investing without undue speculation. We typically seek "bases" in a stock's price patterns with the belief that speculators will not own the stock or be interested in it at that moment. Reading the chart of a stock is often an art, but in today's market it is a necessary skill to complement a fundamental analysis.

10. CATALYST FOR RECOGNITION.

To maximize total return for clients, we not only look for undervalued securities, but try to anticipate events that will close the gap between a stock's price and its intrinsic value. Such an event may be a repurchase plan of a sizable number of outstanding shares, new products, increased merger activity within the industry, the redeployment of assets, margin expansion, new technology, new service, reduced cost factors, etc.

Biography: Denison grew up in the securities business, having spent many of his adolescent years working at the H.C. Denison Company, a brokerage firm that his father founded and ran for over 50 years.

Following his graduation from Lawrence University in 1968, where he was elected to Phi Beta Kappa and was a Rhodes Scholar nominee, he spent nearly four years as an officer in the U.S. Navy. Before joining the Milwaukee Company as director of research in 1985, he spent 13 years in the mechanical contracting business, initially operating his own successful firm and later serving as chief financial officer of one of the largest companies in the industry. While at the Milwaukee Company, his research department developed a reputation for delivering superior value-oriented stock recommendations to clients of the firm.

In 1988, following the merger of the Milwaukee Company into Dain Bosworth, he joined Bill Nasgowitz at Heartland Advisors. He is responsible for directing Heartland's in-house research activities, as well as managing private accounts and comanaging the Heartland Value Fund.

Denison was born in Sheboygan and now lives in Shorewood with his wife and son. He is a trustee of the DeLand Foundation.

Richard Fentin

PORTFOLIO MANAGER

FIDELITY PURITAN, FIDELITY INVESTMENTS, BOSTON

Assets under management: $10 billion

Years of investment experience: 15

Strategy: Value investor. "Buy stocks when others don't want to own them. Buy stocks early (fundamentally) based on value. Sell early, also."

Biography: Born in 1955 in Wilmington, Delaware, Fentin was a loan officer with Peoples Bank & Trust Company before joining Fidelity in 1980.

Mario J. Gabelli

CHAIRMAN AND CHIEF INVESTMENT OFFICER

GAMCO INVESTORS AND GABELLI FUNDS, RYE, NEW YORK

Assets under management: GAMCO: $4.3 billion; Gabelli Funds, $4.1 billion

Years of investment experience: 30

Strategy: "We buy the stocks of cash-generating, franchise-like (dominant market share) companies selling at a deep discount to our fundamental appraisal of their intrinsic value. We also look for a catalyst, an element of change, that will help surface value."

Biography: Mario J. Gabelli is chairman and chief investment officer of GAMCO Investors and Gabelli Funds, adviser to 11 open-end funds and one closed-end fund. Prior to forming the companies that bear his name in 1977, Gabelli served as a securities analyst with Loeb, Rhoades, and William D. Witter. Mr. Gabelli is a *summa cum laude* graduate of Fordham University and received an M.B.A. from Columbia Graduate School of Business. He is frequently quoted in the financial press, and a member of *Barron's* prestigious year-end Roundtable. He has made numerous appearances on "Louis Rukeyser's Wall $treet Week".

Peter S. Hagerman

MANAGING DIRECTOR

HALLMARK CAPITAL MANAGEMENT

Assets under management: $240 million

Years of investment experience: 30

Strategy: Buying growth as well as undervalued stocks.

Biography: A cofounder and managing director of Hallmark, he was previously the director and chief operating officer of Hutton Capital Management, a division of E.F. Hutton and Company. He founded that division for the firm in 1978. Before that he was an investment counselor with Estabrook & Company.

He received a B.S. in business administration from Lehigh University and an M.B.A. in investments from New York University.

Richard S. Huson

CO-FOUNDER, VICE PRESIDENT, AND CHIEF INVESTMENT OFFICER

THE CRABBE HUSON GROUP, PORTLAND

Assets under management: $1.9 billion

Years of investment experience: 27

Strategy: "While fundamentals (price-sales, price-book value, yield, earnings) establish the price of stocks over long time periods, 5 to 10 to 15 years, investor attitudes establish short-term trends and turning points. We try to get a handle on how investors will react to known information in this efficient environment, where most of us are talking to the same people at the same time and getting roughly the same information."

Biography: Before cofounding The Crabbe Huson Company in 1980, Huson was, for three years, a registered representative at Foster & Marshall, where he worked with Crabbe. From 1974–77, he was senior vice-president, investment director, and portfolio manager of the $1.5 billion Boston Company Institutional Investors. Huson previously managed mutual funds with Wellington Management Company (Boston) and Financial Programs (now Invesco) in Denver. He began his career in investments as a securities analyst after earning a B.S. in finance and economics from Portland State University in 1966. He is a Chartered Financial Analyst.

Warren Isabelle

PORTFOLIO MANAGER

PIONEER CAPITAL GROWTH, BOSTON

Assets under management: $1.1 billion

Years of investmemt experience: 12

Strategy: Aggressive value.

Biography: Born in 1952 in Gardner, Massachusetts, Isabelle studied chemistry at the University of Lowell and received an M.S. from the University of Massachusetts in 1980. A Chartered Financial Analyst, he joined the Pioneering Management Corporation in 1984.

Arnold M. Kaufman

EDITOR AND PUBLISHER, STANDARD & POOR'S *THE OUTLOOK*

Assets under management: N.A.

Years of investment experience (at Standard & Poor's): 25

Strategy: "Researching carefully. Monitoring closely. Not averse to taking losses."

Biography: Vice president of Standard & Poor's Corporation. He writes *The Outlook's* weekly market forecast and investment-strategy column. He is also publisher of two newsletters dealing with legal regulations and a dividend-reinvestment guide. He is S&P's spokesman on dividend trends and vice chairman of the company's investment policy committee.

Kaufman joined S&P in 1960 and held a variety of positions before being named *Outlook* editor in 1973. A graduate of Baruch College, he has an M.B.A. in finance and investment from New York University.

Warren Lammert

MANAGER

JANUS MERCURY, DENVER

Assets under management: $3.5 billion

Years of investment experience (at Janus): 7

Strategy: "Bottom-up, research-intensive stock-picking, focused on finding earnings growth at a discount. My success depends on (1) effective research, (2) discipline on p/e multiples on both the buy and sell side, (3) willingness to admit mistakes and sell stocks."

Biography: Born in St. Louis in 1962, Lammert studied economics at Yale and obtained an M.S. in economics from the London School of Economics in 1989. He was a securities analyst at Janus Capital in 1987 and 1988, left to study in London, then returned in 1990. From 1984 to 1986 he was an analyst with Fred Alger Management. He is a Chartered Financial Analyst.

William J. Lippman/Bruce C. Baughman

SENIOR VICE PRESIDENT

TEMPLETON/FRANKLIN ADVISERS

Assets under management: $900 million

Years of investment experience: 34

Strategy: "We try to select decent companies with good management selling below tangible book value. Careful research and analysis of the balance sheet. In general, we try to buy a dollar's worth of value for eighty cents."

Biographies: William J. Lippman is president and director of Franklin

Managed Trust, which includes Franklin Rising Dividends, Franklin Corporate Qualified Dividend, and Investment Grade Income Fund. He also manages Franklin Balance Sheet Investment, Franklin Valuemark Rising Dividends Fund, and the affiliated Hampton Utilities Trust.

Before joining Franklin, Lippman was president of L.F. Rothschild Fund Management. From 1960 to 1986 he was president of Pilgrim Group, a firm that he founded. He is also a former member of the board of trustees of the Investment Company Institute.

Lippman graduated *cum laude* with a B.B.A. from City College in New York City and holds a master's degree in business administration from New York University.

Bruce C. Baughman is co-portfolio manager for the Franklin Rising Dividends Fund, Franklin Balance Sheet Investment, and Hampton Utilities Trust. Before joining Franklin in 1988 he served as a portfolio manager with L.F. Rothschild and the Pilgrim Group. A Certified Public Accountant, Baughman holds a B.A. degree in English from Stanford University and an M.S. degree in accounting from New York University. He is a member of the American Institute of Certified Public Accountants and the New York State Society of Certified Public Accountants.

Thomas F. Marsico

VICE PRESIDENT

JANUS CAPITAL

PORTFOLIO MANAGER FOR THE JANUS TWENTY FUND AND JANUS GROWTH AND INCOME FUND, MARSICO IS ALSO PORTFOLIO MANAGER FOR SEPARATE MANAGED ACCOUNTS AND THE IDEX GROUP OF MUTUAL FUNDS.

Assets under management: $7.0 billion

Years of investmnet experience: 17

Strategy: "I like to invest in companies with strong unit growth and/ or companies in which the fundamentals are improving as a result of a favorable change (i.e, new product, new management, divestiture, reorganization). I like companies with capable management and strong market position."

Biography: Before joining Janus Capital in April 1986, Marsico was senior portfolio manager with Fred Alger Management in New York and a partner with Boettscher and Company. He received his undergraduate degree from the University of Colorado, Boulder, and a master's degree in finance from the University of Denver.

Terry Milberger

SENIOR PORTFOLIO MANAGER

SECURITY MANAGEMENT, TOPEKA, KANSAS

Assets under management: $2 billion

Years of investment experience: 20

Strategy: "Being flexible in investment approach. The ability to use a blend of growth and value investments to take advantage of relative risk/rewards of each sector."

Biography: Born in 1948, he received a B.S. in business from the University of Kansas in 1970 and an M.B.A. in 1972. He has worked for Security Management since 1974, and is a Chartered Financial Analyst.

Gary Pilgrim

CHIEF EXECUTIVE OFFICER, PRESIDENT

PILGRIM BAXTER & ASSOCIATES, WAYNE, PENNSYLVANIA

Assets under management: $3.0 billion

Years of investment experience: 25

Strategy: "Disciplined approach to stock selection criteria through all market conditions."

Biography: Born in 1940 in Nevada, Oklahoma, Pilgrim received a B.A. in business administration from the University of Tulsa in 1967 and an M.B.A. in finance from Drexel in 1971. He spent 15 years as chief investment officer with Philadelphia National Bank before becoming chief investment officer of Pilgrim Baxter & Associates. He is a Chartered Financial Analyst.

Michael F. Price

PRESIDENT

MUTUAL SERIES FUND, INC., SHORT HILLS, NEW JERSEY

Assets under management: $7.7 billion

Years of investment experience: 20

Strategy: "Combination of value investing, trading in stocks involved in mergers, tenders, and bankruptcy situations."

Biography: After obtaining a degree in finance from the University of

Oklahoma in 1973, he joined Max Heine and the Mutual Shares Corporation in 1975.

Douglas D. Ramos

VICE PRESIDENT AND SENIOR PARTNER

NEW ENGLAND BALANCED FUND

LOOMIS, SAYLES & CO., BOSTON

Assets under management: $1.3 billion

Years of investment experience: 15

Strategy: "I focus on the low p/e area of the market. My primary interest is companies selling at below-market p/e ratios with above-average projected earnings-per-share growth. In addition, I try to build investment portfolios with above-average return on equities, below-average payout ratios, and above-average projected dividend growth."

Biography: Ramos began his career as an analyst in the trust division of a New York money-center bank. In 1985 after having moved to Los Angeles and before joining Loomis, Sayles, he was a trust officer and portfolio manager in the Los Angeles office of a major bank. He received a B.A. from the University of Rhode Island in 1980 and became a Chartered Financial Analyst in 1987.

Brian C. Rogers

MANAGER

T. ROWE PRICE EQUITY INCOME

T. ROWE PRICE ASSOCIATES, BALTIMORE

Assets under management: $4 billion

Years of investment experience: 13

Strategy: "Relative valuation analyses focusing on identification of historically inexpensive, yield-oriented stocks."

Biography: Rogers is a managing director and portfolio manager for T. Rowe Price Associates, responsible for several of the firm's major separate-account portfolios. He also serves as president of T. Rowe Price Equity Income Fund and the T. Rowe Price Dividend Growth Fund. Before joining the fund in 1982, Rogers was employed by Bankers Trust Company as a loan officer and credit analyst. He earned an A.B. degree from Harvard College and an M.B.A. from Harvard Business School. He has achieved the Chartered Financial Analyst and Chartered Investment Counselor accreditations.

Eileen Rominger

SENIOR VICE PRESIDENT

OPPENHEIMER CAPITAL/QUEST FOR VALUE

Assets under management: $30 billion (firm)

Years of investment experience: 13

Strategy: Focus on free cash flow return on investment. Look for businesses with powerful industrial positions. Extensive contact with managements to determine plans for creating shareholder value.

Biography: Born in White Plains, New York, Rominger studied at Fairfield University, then obtained an M.B.A. in finance from Wharton in 1981, the same year she joined Oppenheimer Capital.

Robert Sanborn

PORTFOLIO MANAGER

OAKMARK FUND, CHICAGO

PRINCIPAL, HARRIS ASSOCIATES, CHICAGO

Assets under management: $1.4 billion

Years of investment experience: 11

Strategy: "We have five guidelines: (1) Price in market much less than the underlying value; (2) owner-oriented management; (3) trade infrequently; (4) do not overdiversify; and (5) think independently. Our edge lies in these areas: (1) an investment (not marketing) culture; (2) low turnover of key people; and (3) disciplined execution of our investment philosophy."

Biography: Born in 1958 in Boston, Sanborn studied at Dartmouth, then received an M.B.A. from the University of Chicago. He joined Harris Associates in 1988. He earned a Chartered Financial Analyst designation in 1986.

Peter C. Schliemann

MANAGER

SHADOW STOCK, ENTERPRISE, AND ENTERPRISE II FUNDS

DAVID L. BABSON & CO., BOSTON

Assets under management: $750 million

Years of investment experience: 24

Strategy: "David L. Babson & Co. emphasizes a low-risk, fundamental approach to small-company investing. Value is added through our stock-selection process. We find neglected companies with strong business franchises and the potential for earnings acceleration that are largely unappreciated by the market. Unlike most managers, we look for companies with currently depressed margins and profitability, but with potential to return to average or above-average performance level. By buying stocks that are largely neglected by institutional investors and Wall Street analysts, and that have temporarily depressed earnings, we can invest in high-quality companies at inexpensive relative valuations."

Biography: Born in 1945 in New Haven, Schliemann received a B.A. from Amherst in 1967 and an M.B.A. from Harvard in 1969. He joined David L. Babson & Co. in 1979. Prior to that he had spent nine years as a securities analyst with the Boston Company.

Ralph L. Seger Jr.

CHAIRMAN

SEGER-ELVEKROG INC., BLOOMFIELD HILLS

Assets under management: $30 million

Years of investment experience: 40

Biography: A Chartered Financial Analyst, Seger is a trustee of the National Association of Investment Clubs and a member of the securities review and editorial advisory committee of NAIC's *Better Investing* magazine.

He has written the popular "Repair Shop" column in *Better Investing* since 1962. Since 1974, he has operated the NAIC Investor Advisory Service for the National Association of Investment Clubs. He received a B.S. in chemical engineering and an MBA.

Sandra Shrewsbury

MANAGER

PIPER JAFFRAY EMERGING GROWTH, MINNEAPOLIS

Assets under management:

Years of investment experience:

Strategy: Buying small company stocks.

Biography: Born in 1947 in Auburn, Nebraska, Shrewsbury studied at Nebraska University and received an M.S. from Iowa State University. She spent a year as an assistant professor of finance at the College of St. Catherine, then three years as an assistant professor of business administration at Doane College in Crete, Nebraska. She is a Chartered Financial Analyst.

Richard S. Strong

PORTFOLIO MANAGER

STRONG FUNDS

Assets under management: $10.3 billion

Years of investment experience: 29

Strategy: "We're looking for companies with capable, hungry managements that have proprietary or semi-proprietary products in rapidly
growing markets. We want companies that are growing rapidly by
producing more units rather than increasing prices. We would like
to find these qualities in a company selling for an earnings multiple
at a meaningful discount to its growth rate.

"We also look for attractive cash margins, preferably double digit,
so that the company can self-finance a rapid growth rate (20 percent
or better). Our edge is our expertise and experience in growth-stock
investing and a disciplined work ethic.

"I still love the business and work as hard as ever. And because
the world is changing as fast or faster than ever, there are always
opportunities for investors willing to embrace change by investing
in companies with new or better ways of adding value to our
economic system."

Biography: Born in 1942, Strong studied at Baldwin-Wallace College and
received an M.B.A. in finance from the University of Wisconsin. He
managed portfolios for Nicholas, Strong & Company, which he
helped establish in 1967. He founded Strong/Corneliuson Capital
Management in 1974.

Heiko H. Thieme

CHIEF EXECUTIVE OFFICER

AMERICAN HERITAGE MANAGEMENT, NEW YORK CITY

Assets under management: $100 million

Years of investment experience: 20

Strategy: "I see up to 400 companies a year and follow up on their news
on a quarterly basis."

Biography: After receiving a law degree from the University of
Hamburg, Thieme worked as a senior executive with Wood &
McKenzie, as vice president of marketing with White Weld, and as
executive vice president with Deutsche Bank Capital Corporation.
He took over the American Heritage Fund in 1990.

Peter Van Dyke, Ph.D.

MANAGING DIRECTOR

T. ROWE PRICE ASSOCIATES, BALTIMORE

Assets under management: $3 billion

Years of investment experience: 25

Strategy: "Diversify. And look for good management in a growth area without cut-throat competition."

Biography: President of the T. Rowe Price Spectrum Income Fund, Spectrum Growth Fund, Personal Strategy Fund Series, GNMA Fund, U.S. Treasury Long-Term Fund, Adjustable Rate U.S. Government Fund, and CUNA U.S. Government and Cornerstone Funds. Author of, and responsible for, the firm's quantitative fixed-income investment process, and a vice president of Rowe Price-Fleming International.

Before joining T. Rowe Price in 1985, Van Dyke was a senior engineer with the Johns Hopkins University Applied Physics Laboratory. He also managed stock and real-estate investments for 15 years through a Securities and Exchange Commission-registered investment management company that he had founded. Van Dyke earned a B.S. from the Webb Institute, an S.M. and Ph.D. (applied mathematics) from Harvard University, and an M.S. (management science) from the Johns Hopkins University.

Donald A. Yacktman

PRESIDENT

YACKTMAN ASSET MANAGEMENT, CHICAGO

Assets under management: $430 million

Years of investment experience: 26

Strategy: "(1) Buy good businesses. (2) Shareholder-oriented manage-ment. (3) Low valuation (cheap)."

Yacktman thinks of himself as both a value and growth investor. Many value investors, he believes, buy poor-quality companies simply because of their low prices, then they get lumbered with cheap assets.

The trouble with value investors, in his view, is that they tend to buy and sell too early. "Value investors tend to rely solely on price: They buy as soon as the price drops, and sell as soon as it hits its target price."

As for growth investors: "Too many chase prices"—they buy too high. His view of what distinguishes good investors: "They let the prices come to them.

"We try to go someplace in between."

Biography: Before forming his present firm, Yacktman served for 10 years as the senior portfolio manager at Selected Financial Services, Chicago. He had joined Selected in 1982 from Stein Roe & Farnham, Chicago, where he had been a portfolio manager since 1968 and a partner since 1974.

While at Selected, Yacktman had been the president and portfolio manager of the Selected American Shares fund from January 1, 1983, to March 6, 1992. During his tenure, Selected American had an 18.2 percent annualized total return, compared to 13.5 percent for the average equity mutual fund.

Yacktman holds a B.A. *magna cum laude* in economics from the University of Utah and an M.B.A. with distinction from Harvard University. He is also a member of Phi Beta Kappa. He lives in the Chicago suburb of Arlington Heights with his wife, Carolyn, and five of their seven children.

Chapter 6

How Many Stocks Should You Own?

O ne interesting study has concluded that you must own at least 20 stocks to avoid your portfolio's underperforming the Standard & Poor's 500 Stock Index. ("The Law of Small Numbers," John K. Ford, *AAII Journal*, January 1990.)

But the typical panelist, of the 30 polled for this book, believes that 10 to 15 stocks may be enough.

Growth investors—those who invest in the stocks of companies whose earnings are rising—preferred 10 to 15 stocks; value investors, who look for undervalued stocks, recommended 15 to 20. (See Chapter 3 for a discussion of growth versus value investing.)

One reason why growth investors vote for fewer stocks may be that it requires more effort to follow the stocks of growing companies. You must be poised to sell as soon as the earnings begin to slow. Besides, as value panelist Bruce Baughman has said, you can become bored waiting for value stocks to rebound. And the more stocks you own, the more likely something interesting will happen to at least one stock you own—and the less bored you will be.

The question that the panelists were asked was: What is the minimum number of stocks that the average investor should own for adequate diversification?

Art Bonnell: 10 to 15

Rudy Carryl: 10 to 15

Robert Christensen: 15 to 20

James Craig: 15 to 20

Maureen Cullinane: below 10

Hugh Denison: 10 to 15

Richard Fentin: 10 to 15

Mario Gabelli: More than 30

Peter Hagerman: 15 to 20

Richard Huson: More than 20

Warren Isabelle: More than 20

Arnold Kaufman: NA

Warren Lammert: 15 to 20

William Lippman/Bruce Baughman: "Depends on size of the account."

Thomas Marsico: 10 to 15

Terry Milberger: More than 30

Gary Pilgrim: More than 30.

Michael Price: "Depends on amount of money and who the investor is."

Douglas Ramos: More than 20.

Brian Rogers: 10 to 15

Eileen Rominger: 15 to 20

Robert Sanborn: 10 to 15

Peter Schliemann: 15 to 20

Ralph Seger: 10 to 15

Sandra Shrewsbury: 15 to 20

Richard Strong: More than 20

Heiko Thieme: 10 to 15

Peter Van Dyke: 10 to 15

Donald Yacktman: 10 to 15

Panelists responding: 28

Average: Closer to 10–15 (11 votes) than to 15–20 (7 votes). Four panelists voted for over 20, three for over 30, one for fewer than 10.

Median: 15–20.

Contrarians: Cullinane (below 10), Pilgrim (over 30), Gabelli (over 30), Millberger (over 30)

Growth investors, 10–15 (Cullinane was lowest, with fewer than 10) versus value investors, 15–20

Here are some of the panelists' comments.

Bonnel (10 to 15): "If you take a statistics course, you'll find that 15 is a fairly good sample, which will give you a normal standard deviation [a measure of risk or volatility]. Spreading investment risk over a great number of stocks minimizes the risk associated with the individual stocks, but doesn't have the potential to generate as good a return."

Pilgrim (more than 30): "You should have different styles of money management making up your asset structure. That's more important than the number of stocks you own."

Strong (more than 20): "A 2 percent position in any investment is a major position. Things can go wrong with a company, no matter how good it is."

Chapter 7

How Good Do You Have to Be?

Peter Lynch, the noted investor, has said that he's happy if 60 percent of the stocks he buys make good money for him.

That seems to be par: Skillful investors choose winning stocks about 60 percent of the time. Presumably this doesn't mean that 40 percent of the time skillful investors choose stocks that proved to be disastrous. The remainder of their choices may be merely adequate performers; only a few are bombs.

It's hard to determine what percentage of any stock portfolio are winners and losers because the definitions are tricky. A stock may be a winner the first year, a loser the second year, a winner the third year. As one panelist asked, "What time period are you considering?" (Our assumption was: the percentage of stocks that were successful during the entire time they were held.)

We told our panelists that a stock with a gain of over 15 percent a year was a good selection, and a stock with a loss of over 15 percent a year was a dog. (Over the years, the stock market seems to return 10–11 percent a year. A 15 percent return is clearly better than average.)

Our panelists reported that their successful choices ranged from 50 percent ("or less") of their selections to 80 percent. Certain universally admired investors among our panelists reported that they were both near the top in their wise choices (Craig, with 70 percent) and at the bottom (Fentin, with 50 percent). Richard Strong reported that only 10 percent to 20 percent of his selections did very well.

The median percentage of successful choices: 60 percent.

The choices of value investors were validated a median of 60 percent of the time. Only one value investor achieved a percentage as high as 70 percent.

Surprisingly, growth investors reported that their choices were on

the money a median of 65 percent of the time. Four of 11 growth
investors said that their stocks were successful 70 percent or more of
the time. (Earlier, we noted that Craig reported that his choices were
corroborated 70 percent of the time; Fentin's were only 50 percent.
Craig is a growth investor, Fentin a value investor.)

Perhaps there really isn't any significant difference in the percentage
of the panelists' choices that work out well and those that don't, despite
our findings.

Then again, perhaps growth investors are successful more often, but
value players make bigger gains per stock. That would make sense
because (1) value investors tend to hold their stocks longer and (2) the
evidence, dating back to 1975, is that value investors do better than
growth investors. On the other hand, since 1980, growth mutual funds
have decisively outperformed value mutual funds (see Chapter 3).

**What percentage of your stock selections return a good profit (over
15 percent) in a year?**

Art Bonnel: 65%

Rudy Carryl: 65%

Robert Christensen: 50%

James Craig: 70%

Maureen Cullinane: 70%

Hugh Denison: 60%

Richard Fentin: 50%

Mario Gabelli: "Not a viable question."

Peter Hagerman: 60% (on average in a year)

Richard Huson: 65%

Warren Isabelle: 60%

Arnold Kaufman: 55%

Warren Lammert: 65%

William Lippman/Bruce Baughman: "Don't know."

Thomas Marsico: 50%

Terry Milberger: 70%

Gary Pilgrim: 60%

Michael Price: "Don't know."

Douglas Ramos: 50%

Brian Rogers: 70%

Eileen Rominger: 60%

Robert Sanborn: 60%

Peter Schliemann: 50% or less

Ralph Seger: 80% ("Over a five-year period.")

Sandra Shrewsbury: 50%

Richard Strong: 10–20%

Heiko Thieme: 80% ("Impossible to measure.")

Peter Van Dyke: 50%

Donald Yacktman: 50%

As for the percentage of their choices that prove unfortunate, the median the panelists reported was 5 percent to 10 percent. The low was 5 percent or less, the high was 20 percent to 30 percent (Fentin, Lammert, and Ramos). Fentin, a remarkably successful investor, was thus in the money 50 percent of the time and out of the money 20 to 30 percent of the time. That seems to answer the question: How good do you have to be? Be right about twice as often as you are wrong.

Segar and Thieme sustained serious losses only 10–20 percent of time, a ratio of from four to nine winners to every loser.

A few investors reported that they were successful 70 percent of the time, unsuccessful only 5–10 percent of the time (Craig, Cullinane, Millberger, Rogers). That's a ratio of 14 or 7 to 1.

Those whose choices didn't pan out only 5 percent of the time, or less, didn't necessarily have an unusually high percentage of winners. They seem to have invested in many mediocrities.

Carryl reported that his own selections worked out 65 percent of the time, and did poorly only 5 percent of the time or less, a ratio of 13 to 1.

Did growth investors suffer more grievous wounds than value investors? The median growth investor was seriously hurt by 10 percent to 20 percent of his or her selections. Two were hurt only 5 percent of the time or less.

The median for value investors was lower: 5 percent to 10 percent.

Two value investors were hurt only 5 percent of the time or less, but two of the three highest percentages of losses—20 percent to 30 percent—were reported by value investors. So the evidence seems inconclusive.

But of investors with high ratios of winners to losers, there were five growth players to one value player. And, as mentioned, the panelist with the worst ratio was a value investor, Fentin.

Inconsiderately, blend investors—those who invest across the board—didn't resolve the problem. Their profitable trades occurred 65 percent of the time, their unprofitable trades 5 percent to 10 percent of the time.

What percentage of your stock selections lead to a sizable loss (over 15 percent) in a year?

Art Bonnel: 10 to 20%

Rudy Carryl: 5% or less

Robert Christensen: 5 to 10%

James Craig: 5 to 10%

Maureen Cullinane: 5 to 10%

Hugh Denison: 10 to 20%

Richard Fentin: 20 to 30%

Mario Gabelli: "not a viable question"

Peter Hagerman: 5 to 10%

Richard Huson: 5 to 10%

Warren Isabelle: 10 to 20%

Arnold Kaufman: 5 to 10%

Warren Lammert: 20 to 30%

William Lippman/Bruce Baughman: "Don't know."

Thomas Marsico: 5 to 10%

Terry Milberger: 5 to 10%

Gary Pilgrim: 10 to 20%

Michael Price: 5% or less

Douglas Ramos: 20 to 30%

Brian Rogers: 5 to 10%

Eileen Rominger: 5% or less
Robert Sanborn: 5 to 10%
Peter Schliemann: 10 to 20%
Ralph Seger: 10 to 20%
Sandra Shrewsbury: 10 to 20%
Richard Strong: 10 to 20%
Heiko Thieme: 10 to 20%
Peter Van Dyke: 5% or less
Donald Yacktman: 5% or less

Chapter 8

The Case for Index Investing

Y ou hear on the news that the Dow has plunged almost 100 points. Just how worrisome is it? Or you read that the Dow has risen 53 points. Should you break out the champagne? Call your travel agent?

Many people probably have only the vaguest idea what the Dow Jones Industrial Average, the Standard & Poor's 500, and other famous indexes are. Yet indexes that track your investments' performance give you the information that you need to invest wisely.

First we'll discuss what indexes are. Then we'll describe the most celebrated indexes. Finally we'll explain why people can profit from investing in index funds, portfolios that mirror an index.

You're cooking a stew. You want to know how things are going, so you taste a forkful. Not salty enough; you add more salt.

The stew is like a market—the arena where people buy and sell stocks, bonds, commodities, and so on.

The forkful is like an index—a piece of the market that, you trust, tells you what the entire market is like, just as a forkful should let you know what the entire stew is like (unless the salt somehow didn't spread to the forkful you tasted).

An index is typically a sampling of an entire market. A replica. A mirror. It tells you what an entire market has been doing—going up, down, or sideways.

An enormous number of common stock are being bought and sold all the time—maybe 7,000. If you want to know whether the prices of stocks in general went up or down since yesterday, or since 10 or 50 years ago, you can check what a sampling of stocks has done over whatever time period you're interested in. In 1993, for example, the Standard & Poor's 500 Stock Index rose 10.06 percent.

Why are there so many stock and bond indexes? You may also have heard of the New York Stock Exchange Index, the Wilshire 5000, the Russell 2000, and the Lehman Brothers Aggregate Bond Index.

One answer is that there are a lot of different markets and sub-varieties of markets—utility stocks, real estate investment trusts (REITS), the DAX index of Frankfurt stocks, corporate-bond indexes, junk-bond indexes, and so forth.

Another reason is that many of the indexes have flaws. The Dow Jones Industrial Average (DJIA) is the most famous index, yet almost everyone agrees that it's an imperfect mirror of the stock market, for these reasons:

- It has only 30 stocks.
- They're all gigantic companies.
- The index really is an *average*. The prices of the 30 stocks are divided by a specific number (the "divisor") to produce the average. That means that stocks that happen to be high-priced count more than stocks that happen to be low-priced.
- The Dow exaggerates market movements because the divisor of the average has been decreasing, and that makes the Dow's changes seem bigger than they are. (The divisor decreases because stocks are removed, or split, or provide dividends.) When the DJIA was introduced in 1928, a one-point move in every Dow stock caused a one-point move in the overall average. Today, a one-point change in every Dow stock will push the entire average up or down 76 points.

Sophisticated investors agree that a more reliable monitor of the market is one that uses more stocks than 30, in particular the Standard & Poor's 500 Stock Index. The S&P 500 Stock Index contains 16.66 times as many stocks as the DJIA. Those stocks are "weighted." The value of the company's stock determines how much it influences the index. To determine a stock's value, its price per share is multiplied by the number of shares outstanding, which measures the stock's "capitalization."

But while the DJIA is rude and crude, it does its job of showing what the market has been up to with the clarity that most investors seem to want. Most of the time, the DJIA and the S&P 500 follow each other pretty closely.

Besides, although the S&P 500 is the index used by experienced investors, it, too, has a flaw. It's tilted toward big-company stocks. And if you own small-company stocks, the S&P 500 isn't of much use to you as a model. You might try comparing your portfolio instead to an index of small-company stocks, like the Russell 2000.

Indexes can tell you where a market has been going. If you want to, you can buy stocks when prices are climbing and sell when prices are heading down. Or, if you're a contrarian investor, you can do just the opposite, because you think that when stock prices are low they may be bargains, whereas when they are high they may be expensive.

Whatever type of investment you own, you will also want to know how its performance has compared with that of an index of similar securities. If you own utility stocks, for example, you may be curious to learn whether they have underperformed or outperformed an index of other utility stocks.

But even if your individual stocks or your mutual funds didn't beat a suitable index recently, there can be a good excuse. Perhaps their prices were less volatile, thus sparing you from worrisome flip-flops.

In short, indexes can be useful investment tools—even if their volatility sometimes can be scary.

Index funds have been called the "plain vanilla" of mutual funds. They're simple investments. Yet a lot of investors seem to like them a lot—just as most people like the flavor of vanilla.

If you own an index fund, you need not worry that the portfolio manager may leave, or that he or she may own too many health-care stocks when the health-care sector takes a hit. You don't have to fret that your fund may be incurring exorbitant expenses.

All that an index fund does is buy all (or a representative sample) of the securities in an index of a market, then change the mix as the index itself changes—if, for example, a company merges with another company, or a company issues more shares.

The opposite of an index fund is an actively managed fund.

Most index funds are so well diversified that they will rarely perform fabulously well in any year. But they will also rarely fall on their faces. Over the past 10 years, the Wilshire Index has outperformed 75 percent of stock funds, according to Lipper Analytical Services.

Besides offering diversification and low expenses, an index fund provides these other benefits:

- Shareholders rarely have high capital-gains taxes to pay: The fund doesn't sell stocks very often, so its gains are unrealized and untaxed.
- Even if the fund's assets climb, the fund will be able to cope—unlike funds that invest only in certain types of stocks (like small-company stocks) and that may be handicapped if a flood of new money pours in.
- An index fund doesn't follow just one investment style, such as searching for undervalued or growing stocks. That's why index funds may not be badly hurt if an investment style drifts out of favor for a while.
- You are forced to buy stocks that other investors wouldn't dream of buying except in their nightmares—because they are so far out of favor. The companies have cut their dividends, or are being sued, or have lost key officers. Yet such stocks have a tendency to rebound mightily. Years ago, an investment company in California created an index fund and decided to leave out the obvious dogs. Naturally, enough of the dogs turned into winners so that anyone would have made a princely profit compiling a portfolio of them.
- The manager of an index fund need not keep any money in cash, the way open-ended mutual funds must. He or she can keep fully invested in stocks—and, over the years, being entirely in stocks has plainly been better than being partly in stocks and partly in cash. Open-end actively managed funds must keep some cash on hand to pay off shareholders who want out. An index fund can just sell a variety of its investments.

These days, you can even buy index funds that contain just undervalued stocks, or the stocks of fast-growing companies—investment styles rather than just stocks. Vanguard, as mentioned in Chapter 3, offers both value- and growth-stock indexes.

Index funds are not perfect. For one thing, they can be very volatile. For another, the best-known index funds don't contain many small-company stocks, which over the years have done better than big-company stocks. (Some observers argue that the evidence that small-company stocks have done better comes only from studies of the smallest 10 percent of the stocks on the New York Stock Exchange, and they claim these stocks are not typical of small-company stocks.)

So, while index funds may make sense if you're interested mainly in large-company stocks, you may be better off buying particular small-company stocks on your own. Such stocks aren't that well researched; an investor's choices, therefore, may perform much better than his or her choices of big-company stocks.

In other words, by buying individual small-company stocks (which you can do through an actively managed mutual fund), you have an excellent chance of beating the indexes. Small-company index funds have not done exceptionally well at all, including such funds as DFA 9–10 Small Company and Vanguard Index Small Cap Stock.

You can readily buy an index fund. One with no sales charges that broadly emulates the Dow Jones Industrial Average is ASM Fund, which has a $1,000 minimum (phone: 800-445-2763). But the best source of index funds is the Vanguard family in Valley Forge, Pennsylvania. Whatever index you have in mind, Vanguard probably offers a replica.

Here are the Vanguard index funds and their Morningstar rankings and ratings versus funds with similar objectives as of April 1995:

Fund	Ranking	(years)	Rating
Vanguard Balanced Index	32/199	(1 year)	
Vanguard Bond Index Intermediate-Term Bond	40/318	(1 year)	
Vanguard Bond Index Long-Term Bond	34/318	(1 year)	
Vanguard Bond Index Short-Term Bond	653/318	(1 year)	
Vanguard Bond Index Total Bond Market	36/93	(5 years)	****
Vanguard Index 500	17/106	(10 years)	****
Vanguard Index Extended Market	59/92	(5 years)	****
Vanguard Index Growth	25/662	(1 year)	
Vanguard Index Small Cap-Stock	37/42	(10 years)	***
Vanguard Index Total Stock Market	111/357	(1 year)	
Vanguard Index Value	132/357	(1 year)	
Vanguard Institutional Index	53/227	(3 years)	****

Fund	Ranking	(years)	Rating
Vanguard Intl Equity Index			
Emerging Markets	253/298	(3 months)	
Vanguard Intl Equity Index			
European	6/23	(3 years)	****
Vanguard Intl Equity Index			
Pacific	8/22	3 years)	****

Source: Morningstar, April 1995.

A rating of four stars is above average; three stars is average.

Interestingly, index funds don't always beat the competition. As mentioned, small-company index funds don't do as well as most small-company funds—because, the explanation goes, small companies aren't followed so carefully by Wall Street analysts, and analysts can discover underpriced gems.

You might expect the same to be true of foreign stock funds, but George Sauter, who runs Vanguard's index funds, reports that they generally don't do as well as the indexes, perhaps because of the high cost of doing research abroad.

Buying a large-company index fund is a good approach for someone who doesn't want to devote time and attention to investment markets, yet insists on being conservative and taking advantage of the high returns of the stock market. Such an investor need only buy Vanguard Balanced Index Fund, or buy both Vanguard Total World Index plus Vanguard Balanced Index Fund in whatever percentages seem comfortable. (For a young person, that might be 70 percent in stocks, 30 percent in bonds.) The investor might rebalance the funds when they go seriously out of whack, such as being off by 10 percent from their original weighting.

Chapter 9

The Case for a Stock Unit Investment Trust

A unit investment trust (UIT) is a portfolio of securities (usually bonds) that are intended to be unchanging. A UIT just buys and holds until the bonds mature, or (in the case of stocks) until a distribution date. All you're getting is a diversified, presumably well-chosen portfolio—not active management.

The case for UITs (of stocks) is similar to the case for investing in index funds.

A UIT is sort of a custom-made index fund, though typically not so diversified.

Another name for the UIT strategy might be the Warren Buffett strategy: Like Buffett, the Sage of Omaha, you buy the stocks of fine companies and hang on. The Buffett strategy, the wisdom of which has been vindicated by the impressive performance of the Berkshire Hathaway company that Buffett manages, differs from the index-fund strategy in that the portfolio isn't nicely diversified. It is *targeted*. In effect, Buffett manages a custom-made index fund, not one ready-to-wear.

That's what investors might do with the 25 stocks recommended by the experts for this book—create a Buffett-like, unit-trust portfolio, and hang on.

The arguments for buying or creating a stock UIT are:

- You have very low transaction fees and administrative costs—as is the case with an index fund.

- You have little in the way of capital-gains taxes to pay because you will rarely, if ever, sell, and you are not taxed on unrealized gains.

- You can pick and choose your stocks—which is not the case with an index fund. And, by being choosy, you might outperform an index fund.

- If you choose blue-chip stocks, you can be pretty certain that most of them will endure and some even excel. You can probably rest assured that, as is the case with most professionally managed portfolios, 60 percent of your selections should do well.
- You don't have the worries thatcome with an actively managed open-end mutual fund, such as that the successful manager might leave, the shareholders get spooked and start selling... and the manager be forced to unload good, cheap securities or that shareholders might get euphoric and start buying, and the manager might have to buy not-so-good, not-so-cheap securities, or keep large sums in cash equivalents.

  With a closed-end fund, which is really a stock, you need not worry about shareholders' panicking and forcing the managers to sell good, cheap securities. But you might worry about your closed-end fund selling at an increasingly greater discount. (Many closed-end funds do trade at discounts to their underlying worth.)
- Companies thrive, decline, thrive, decline, and so on. If you hold on for many years, you can sell when prices are unusually high. Otherwise, you must try to buy companies when they are under a cloud and sell when the sun is shining (the value strategy), or buy when companies are healthy and sell when they begin developing symptoms of illness (the growth strategy). Doing either one accurately and consistently is tough. But just buying healthy companies and holding on may be a satisfactory alternative.

A chief argument against a UIT of stocks is that they are redolent of the Nifty Fifty, a group of stocks that certain investors touted in the 1950s as "one-decision stocks," securities to buy and hold forever—despite their price/earnings ratios of 70, 80, and (in the case of Polaroid) over 90. "It was so easy to forget that probably no sizable company could possibly be worth over 50 times normal earnings," opined *Forbes* magazine (1977).

I myself have heaped scorn on the notion of the Nifty Fifty, writing (in 1989) that "This silly strategy flourished in the late 1960s and early 1970s, and stocks like Avon Products, IBM, and Xerox Corp., soared to the skies, sporting lofty price/earnings ratios. When the cycle turned, the Nifty Fifty came crashing back to earth. Disney went from $27 a share in 1973 to $4 a year later."

Morgan Guaranty Trust has identified a close approximation of the Nifty Fifty. The 50 companies included drugs, computers, electronics, photography, food, tobacco, retailing, and so forth. There were no cyclical (value) stocks: No autos, steels, transportation, capital goods, oils.

In his book, *Stocks for the Long Run* (Irwin Professional Publishing), Jeremy J. Siegel of the Wharton School notes that, in 1993, some 15 of the 50 stocks were among the top 40 companies in the country, and four (General Electric, Coca-Cola, Merck, and Philip Morris) were among the top 10.

The Nifty Fifty's average price/earnings ratio in 1972 was 37.3, more than twice that of the S&P 500. Their average dividend yield was 1.1 percent, less than half of that of other large-company stocks.

Siegel tracked the Nifty Fifty's subsequent performance, taking into consideration corporate changes like mergers. He then created a Nifty Fifty portfolio, and rebalanced it every year so that each stock kept its 2 percent allocation (remaining part of the 50).

From then to 1993, the drug stocks in particular did wonderfully, outperforming the S&P 500 Index. The biggest winners, in order, were Philip Morris, McDonald's, PepsiCo., Disney, and Schlumberger. The biggest losers were MGIC Investment, Emery Air Freight, and Burroughs.

The professor's conclusions: "From January 1972 to May 1993, the return on the Nifty Fifty beats the S&P 500 Index, but falls behind if measured from January 1973 and 1974." That suggests that the returns are pretty close, depending on when you invested your money. "However, from the depth of the bear market in October 1974, the rebalanced portfolio again beats the S&P 500 Index."

A rebalanced portfolio, of course, isn't a UIT. It would have been interesting to compare just the Nifty Fifty with the S&P 500. I suspect that it would have done better than the rebalanced portfolio—by not limiting the appreciation of certain stocks.

Siegel's conclusion: "Did the Nifty Fifty become overvalued during the buying spree of 1972? Yes—but not by much, and by some criteria, not at all!"

In fact, even when you take taxes into consideration, from January 1973 the returns of the Nifty Fifty exceeded that of the S&P 500 Index— except for people in the very lowest tax bracket.

What should the price/earnings ratios of the Nifty Fifty have been?

"In 1972 these stocks were not significantly overvalued on the basis of their subsequent earnings."

In fact, certain glamour stocks, it turned out, were worth more than their lofty p/e ratios in 1972. Investors should have paid 89.1 times earnings for Philip Morris instead of the 21 they did pay. Coca-Cola, PepsiCo, and Disney deserved p/e ratios of 70 or more. McDonald's, which had a multiple of 59.8 at the time, deserved a p/e ratio of 92.2—and 126.3 if calculated on an after-tax basis!

The Nifty Fifty are vindicated.

Eleven of this book's Top 25—nearly half—are among the Nifty Fifty:

Coca-Cola, Philip Morris, 3M, General Electric, IBM, Bristol-Myers and Squibb (which merged into Bristol-Myers Squibb), PepsiCo, Citicorp, McDonald's, Merck, and Pfizer.

A final argument for stock UITs is Lexington Corporate Leaders, a unit investment trust of stocks managed in Saddle Brook, New Jersey.

The fund was launched in 1935, when the managers bought 30 stocks, determining to hold them into the Twenty-First Century. "By charter, we cannot change our holdings," says Larry Cantor, managing director of Lexington Management Corp., "although we can eliminate a stock that no longer meets our criteria."

As an idea, it wasn't half bad. In 1994 LCL made the Forbes Honor Roll of best mutual funds, and its average rating from Morningstar, Inc., has been four stars (above average). As of this writing, it gets five stars, Morningstar's highest rating.

LCL is one of the oddest funds in existence. Among other things, when any of its stocks split, it automatically sells the extra shares! The reason is that LCL must own a specified list of stocks, and it must own them in equal amounts. So it must have the same number of shares of AT&T as of Westinghouse Electric, even though (as of this writing) AT&T was selling for four times the price of Western Electric.

If any stock splits, or provides more shares instead of cash as dividends, LCL must sell some of the new shares—half, if there's been a two-for-one split. As for ordinary cash dividends, they accumulate in a special account until turned over to shareholders. (Most of whom reinvest the money.)

If you had looked at the portfolio in 1995, you might have been appalled. Borden, Columbia Gas, Westinghouse, Woolworth Corp., and three utilities. Only three of the stocks are on this book's list of the 25 best stocks to buy and hold: AT&T, Chevron, General Electric. But here's what the fund has going for it:

- Low expenses. There's no management fee. All that Lexington Management does is boot out any stocks no longer eligible for listing on the New York Stock Exchange, or that stop providing dividends. But, that seldom happens. (Last evicted: Penn Central.)

- A low turnover—lower even than that of an index fund of the S&P 500.

- A portfolio of old-line stocks, some of them very impressive (see the following list).

Which has done better, Vanguard Index Trust 500 or Lexington Corporate Leaders? Over the past 10 years (to the end of 1994), LCL is slightly ahead. Over the past 15 years, too. If you had put $10,000 into the two funds 15 years ago, LCL would have given you $82,040. Vanguard Index 500, only $74,577.

The case for a stock UIT rests.

Stocks in Lexington Corporate Trust

Mobil Corp.
Union Pacific Corp.
The Union Electric Co.
The Travelers Life Insurance Co.
American Brands Inc.
Columbia Gas System
Consolidated Edision of New York
Pacific Gas & Electric
Santa Fe Pacific Corp.
Praxair Inc.
USX-Marathon Group Inc.
Borden Inc.
Chevron Corp.
DuPont
Exxon Corp.
The Procter & Gamble Co.
AT&T Corp.
Sears Roebuck and Co.

The General Electric Co.
The Eastman Kodak Co.
Allied Signal Inc.
Union Carbide Corp.
Woolworth Corp.
Westinghouse Electric Corp.

Chapter 10

Why Only Certain Investors Are Successful

The majority of the panelists polled for this book agreed that the number one requisite for investment success is adhering to your investment strategy. That was the case both among growth investors and value investors.

Obviously, having a strategy in the first place may be even more important than sticking to whatever strategy you choose. And, as one panelist observed, you must have a *good* strategy.

Buying only in January, and being out of the market the remainder of the time, is certainly one strategy, but very likely an ill-advised one. One mutual fund's strategy has been to buy the stocks of companies paying unusually high dividends. The fund has established a mediocre record, suggesting that, as strategies go, this one is rather commonplace.

How our panelists rated other ingredients that contribute to investment success depended in large part on whether they were value, growth, or blend investors.

Not surprisingly, value investors emphasize on the need to be contrarian as an ingredient for success. Growth investors emphasized "being logical and unemotional"—perhaps because they have less time to make decisions. By the same token, they also felt it was unusually important to "pull the trigger quickly and knowledgeably," to buy and sell at the right times.

Both value and growth investors downplayed the contribution of luck to investment success. But growth investors were much more skeptical of luck—perhaps because they work harder and their chances for mistakes are greater. Then again, maybe successful growth investors just don't depend on luck as much as successful value investors do.

Here is how growth investors rated the other various ingredients for investment success:

Growth Investors

2. Being logical and unemotional.

   That may mean everything from "murder your darlings" (as Sir Arthur Quiller-Couch recommended, regarding your favorite prose) to sometimes resisting conventional opinion.
3. Having better research.
4. Following a sell discipline.

   In other words, having a plan that will help you decide when to dump a stock.
5. Experience.

   Presumably, experience teaches you to be cautious. Experienced money managers do seem to be unusually cautious. It may also teach you to avoid traps you've fallen into before.
6. Flexibility.
7. Pulling the trigger quickly and knowledgeably.

Here is how value investors rated various ingredients for success:

Value Investors

2. Having better research.
3. Willingness to be contrarian.
4. Being logical and unemotional.
5. Following a sell discipline.
6. Experience
7. Flexibility.

Ranking the Ingredients

Quality	Average	Growth	Value
Sticking with your strategy	1.10	1.07	1.18
Having better research	1.66	1.7	1.6
Being logical and not emotional	1.69	1.6	1.73

Quality	Average	Growth	Value
Following a sell discipline	1.857	1.727	1.916
Experience	2.07	1.91	2.15
Willingness to be contrarian	2.178	2.63	1.69
Flexibility	2.607	2.36	2.846
Pulling the trigger quickly and knowledgeably	2.86	2.6	3.0
Seeing patterns in rough data	3.10	3.09	3.076
Special statistical guides	3.14	3.1	3.33
Luck	3.41	3.545	3.0

Here are the questions in the success survey, followed by the results —along with commentary from the panelists.

Which of these reasons accounts for someone's success in buying and selling stocks? (Rate from 1, highest, to 5, lowest.)

Sticking with your strategy

Panelist comments:

Sanborn (highest): "You have a philosophy, and you stick with it This is the only way to build a successful business."

Art Bonnel: highest (1)

Rudy Carryl: highest (1)

Robert Christensen: highest (1)

James Craig: highest (1)

Maureen Cullinane: highest (1)

Hugh Denison: highest (1)

Richard Fentin: highest (1)

Mario Gabelli: highest (1)

Peter Hagerman: highest (1)

Richard Huson: highest (1)

Warren Isabelle: highest (1)

Arnold Kaufman: highest (1)

Warren Lammert: highest (1) ("Need right strategy")

William Lippman/Bruce Baughman: highest (1)

Thomas Marsico: highest (1)

Terry Milberger: highest (1)

Gary Pilgrim: highest (1)

Michael Price: highest (1)

Douglas Ramos: highest (1)

Brian Rogers: highest (1)

Eileen Rominger: above average (2)

Robert Sanborn: highest (1)

Peter Schliemann: highest (1)

Ralph Seger: highest (1)

Sandra Shrewsbury: above average (2)

Richard Strong: highest (1)

Heiko Thieme: highest (1)

Peter Van Dyke: above average (2)

Donald Yacktman: highest (1)

Responses: 29
Average: 1.1 (a little below highest)
Median: 1 (highest)
Contrarians: None
Median growth, 1.7, versus median value, 1.6

Pulling the trigger quickly and knowledgeably

Panelist comments:

Bonnel (highest): "If you see something changing and you're not happy with it, you should get out. You have to be able to make decisive, quick judgements, and be brave enough to cut your losses, rather than hope for a turnaround. Conversely, when a stock is rising, you have to know when to sell."

Isabelle (average): "Most of the time, it's not necessary to pull the trigger. Investment decisions usually don't have to be made instantly. If you do act quickly, you can destabilize the market, especially if you have a large amount of stock." (That is, you might drive down the price of whatever you're selling and push up the price of whatever you're buying.) "At the same time, it's important to find out any news that's critical, even if you then take some time to digest the information."

Shrewsbury (lowest): "If you sell too quickly, you risk losing the opportunity to make greater profit or to recoup losses. People run like crazy from the opportunity to buy a bargain."

Yacktman (below average): "There's a lot of frictional costs in turning over a stock, like brokerage commissions. Therefore, before committing to buy a stock, you should know what you're doing. Otherwise, what looks like a good buy may be costly. If one makes careful investments more often, one should get better results."

While Yacktman acknowledges that in-and-out investors like G. Kenneth Heebner (CGM Mutual) can be successful, he also says, "I couldn't operate the way that they do. In general, I think of them as speculators, not as investors."

In general, growth investors would seem more likely to emphasize this yardstick, growth stocks usually being more volatile than value stocks and quick decisions therefore being more appropriate. But there was only a slight bias in that direction on the part of growth investors. Perhaps large-cap growth investors are slower on the trigger than small-cap growth investors.

Art Bonnel: highest (1)

Rudy Carryl: highest (1)

Robert Christensen: average (3)

James Craig: highest (1)

Maureen Cullinane: average (3)

Hugh Denison: below average (4)

Richard Fentin: below average (4)

Mario Gabelli: above average (2)

Peter Hagerman: average (3)

Richard Huson: above average (2)

Warren Isabelle: average (3)

Arnold Kaufman: above average (2)

Warren Lammert: average (3) (underscored knowledgeably)

William Lippman/Bruce Baughman: average (3)

Thomas Marsico: average (3)

Terry Milberger: average (3)

Gary Pilgrim: above average (2)

Michael Price: above average (2)

Douglas Ramos: lowest (5)

Brian Rogers: average (3)

Eileen Rominger: below average (4)

Robert Sanborn: average (3)

Peter Schliemann: above average (2)

Ralph Seger: below average (4)

Sandra Shrewsbury: lowest (5)

Richard Strong: highest (1)

Heiko Thieme: above average (2)

Peter Van Dyke: lowest (5)

Donald Yacktman: below average (4)

Responses: 29

Average: 2.86 (a little above average)

Contrarians: Van Dyke, Shrewsbury, Ramos (5); Bonnel, Carryl, Craig, Strong (1)

Median growth, 2.6, versus median value, 3

Having better research

Panelist comments:

Sanborn (below average): "The question seems to ask whether it's important to do a lot of research to predict what is going to happen to a stock in the next quarter. To me, it's not worth the expenditure. To roughly predict minor fluctuations over the course of several months—to predict whether the next quarter is going to be up a penny or two—is basically a waste of time."

Shrewsbury (highest): "Of primary importance is the fundamental picture of a company, and one of the fundamental components is management. Also, the environment the company is operating in: What are the growth prospects of the company?"

Pilgrim (lowest): "I don't think the average professional investor can gain a significant edge, a proprietary insight, through so-called research. There is only a limited value in predicting what is going to happen because most stock predictions are notoriously wrong. Still, it's important to know what everybody else knows. The issue I have with research is the idea that `My research is better than anyone else's.' The important thing is a disciplined approach."

Yacktman (below average): "It's not that I don't believe in accumulating knowledge. Ultimately, knowledge will win. It's just that I have no faith in Wall Street analysts being the people to acquire it from."

In general, good research does seem vital, except in instances where a manager, like Pilgrim, uses a strongly mathematically approach to choosing stocks. He is, in effect, interpreting the information that is already available.

Art Bonnel: above average (2)

Rudy Carryl: above average (2)

Robert Christensen: above average (2)

James Craig: highest (1)

Maureen Cullinane: above average (2)

Hugh Denison: above average (2)

Richard Fentin: highest (1)

Mario Gabelli: highest (1)

Peter Hagerman: average (3)

Richard Huson: average (3)

Warren Isabelle: highest (1)

Arnold Kaufman: highest (1)

Warren Lammert: above average (2)

William Lippman/Bruce Baughman: highest (1)

Thomas Marsico: highest (1)

Terry Milberger: average (3)

Gary Pilgrim: lowest (5)

Michael Price: highest (1)

Douglas Ramos: above average (2)

Brian Rogers: above average (2)

Eileen Rominger: highest (1)

Robert Sanborn: below average (4)

Peter Schliemann: highest (1)

Ralph Seger: highest (1)

Sandra Shrewsbury: highest (1)

Richard Strong: highest (1)

Heiko Thieme: highest (1)

Peter Van Dyke: highest (1)

Donald Yacktman: below average (4)

Responses: 29
Average: 1.82 (a little higher than "above average")
Contrarians: Gary Pilgrim (5), Sanborn and Yacktman (4)
Median growth, 1.7, versus median value, 1.62

Being logical and unemotional

Panelists' comments:

Isabelle (highest): "You can get emotionally tied to these things. You have to be willing to divorce yourself from a stock that is failing, even if you have sympathy for the company and management. Also, if you employ logic, you might identify a company on the verge of bouncing back and expanding; then buying a stock that seems bad may be the way to an easy profit."

Sanborn (highest): "If you're emotional, you tend to make bad decisions."

Growth investors are perhaps less emotional than value investors. They must buy and sell more actively, and hold on to stocks for shorter periods. Value players may get attached to stocks they have been holding for a long time—and upset about finally having to concede defeat. But the poll showed little difference in their responses.

Art Bonnel: highest (1)

Rudy Carryl: above average (2)

Robert Christensen: average (3)

James Craig: highest (1)

Maureen Cullinane: average (3)

Hugh Denison: highest (1)

Richard Fentin: highest (1)

Mario Gabelli: above average (2)

Peter Hagerman: above average (2)

Richard Huson: above average (2)

Warren Isabelle: highest (1)

Arnold Kaufman: highest (1)

Warren Lammert: average (3)

William Lippman/Bruce Baughman: highest (1)

Thomas Marsico: highest (1)

Terry Milberger: above average (2)

Gary Pilgrim: above average (2)

Michael Price: highest (1)

Douglas Ramos: highest (1)

Brian Rogers: above average (2)

Eileen Rominger: highest (1)

Robert Sanborn: highest (1)

Peter Schliemann: highest (1)

Ralph Seger: above average (2)

Sandra Shrewsbury: highest (1)

Richard Strong: highest (1)

Heiko Thieme: above average (2):

Peter Van Dyke: above average (2)

Donald Yacktman: highest (1)

Responses: 29

Average: 1.69 (a little higher than "above average")

Contrarians: None

Median growth, 1.6, versus median value, 1.73

Seeing patterns in rough data

Panelist comments:

Yacktman (below average): "To the degree that it helps you understand the business, that's fine. It depends on what the data are. My
problem is that I feel that people tend to get trapped in minutiae,
spending so much time looking at obscure, technical, micro data that
they miss the big picture."

Someone who can generalize with sparse information may notice
that a certain industry is beginning to do poorly or beginning to
rebound. But many of our panelists didn't think very highly of this

faculty. I suspected that growth investors would stress this skill, because they must make quicker decisions, but this wasn't borne out.

Art Bonnel: average (3)
Rudy Carryl: lowest (5)
Robert Christensen: average (3)
James Craig: highest (1)
Maureen Cullinane: average (3)
Hugh Denison: below average (4)
Richard Fentin: average (3)
Mario Gabelli: below average (4)
Peter Hagerman: below average (4)
Richard Huson: above average (2)
Warren Isabelle: average (3)
Arnold Kaufman: above average (2)
Warren Lammert: average (3)
William Lippman/Bruce Baughman: lowest (5)
Thomas Marsico: average (3)
Terry Milberger: average (3)
Gary Pilgrim: average (3)
Michael Price: below average (4)
Douglas Ramos: average (3)
Brian Rogers: average (3)
Eileen Rominger: average (3)
Robert Sanborn: highest (1)
Peter Schliemann: above average (2)
Ralph Seger: above average (2)
Sandra Shrewsbury: average (3)
Richard Strong: average (3)
Heiko Thieme: average (3)

Peter Van Dyke: lowest (5)

Donald Yacktman: below average (4)

Responses: 29

Average: 3.10 (slightly below average)

Contrarians: Carryl, Van Dyke (5); Craig, Sanborn (1)

Median growth, 3.09, versus median value, 3.076

Luck

Panelist comments:

Bonnel (lowest): "You only get lucky because you're smart. Unless you've done a lot of homework before buying into a stock, luck won't bring you a large profit. You're not at a roulette table."

Isabelle (highest): "If you're a reasonable investor, a little luck helps push you out that envelope. You can't bank on luck alone, but if you set a base for yourself, occasionally something turns up to accelerate your original theme. Sometimes a safe investment turns out to be wonderfully profitable."

Sanborn (highest): "Oakmark funds have the best record of any fund over the past three years. I think that's at least partly due to luck. I know why we've done well, but we're pretty lucky that we've done so well. At one point, Liberty Media made up 12 percent of Oakmark's portfolio. We got into it through hard work. We successfully cultivated the management. What was lucky about the whole deal was that Liberty's stock rose 10 times. Oakmark just happened to be in the right place at the right time."

One might suspect that value investors in particular would dismiss luck as unimportant. But growth investors rated it lower, perhaps because their job is harder and more stressful—and the difference in performance between top performers and poor performers is wider.

Art Bonnel: lowest (5)

Rudy Carryl: lowest (5)

Robert Christensen: lowest (5)

James Craig: lowest (5)

Maureen Cullinane: below average (4)

Hugh Denison: average (3)

Richard Fentin: lowest (5)

Mario Gabelli: below average (4)

Peter Hagerman: lowest (5)

Richard Huson: below average (4)

Warren Isabelle: highest (1)

Arnold Kaufman: above average (2)

Warren Lammert: above average (2)

William Lippman/Bruce Baughman: average (3)

Thomas Marsico: average (3)

Terry Milberger: below average (4)

Gary Pilgrim: average (3)

Michael Price: highest (1)

Douglas Ramos: lowest (5)

Brian Rogers: below average (4)

Eileen Rominger: average (3)

Robert Sanborn: highest (1)

Peter Schliemann: lowest (5)

Ralph Seger: lowest (5)

Sandra Shrewsbury: above average (2)

Richard Strong: lowest (5)

Heiko Thieme: highest (1)

Peter Van Dyke: highest (1)

Donald Yacktman: average (3)

Responses: 29
Average: 3.41 (somewhat below "average")
Contrarians: 10 gave it a 5, 5 gave it a 1—an unusual disparity
Median growth, 3.55, versus median value, 3.0

Following a sell discipline

Panelist comments:

Bonnel (highest): "Fifteen or 20 years ago, I had a client who owned 5,000 airline shares worth $100 each. She had inherited them from her husband, who had worked for the airline. Out of sentimental reasons she was unwilling to sell. In the end the company went bankrupt, and she was out $500,000. All because she had not followed a sell discipline."

Yacktman (below average): "If you buy the kind of stocks I buy, the critical decision is being able to purchase it—it gets you on the escalator. And if you start when the price is low, then as it rises your profits skyrocket. So it's the buying price that's more important than the sell discipline.

"Selling is also important, though. You can do a bit of gin rummy. But you have to be careful. If you gamble too much on when to sell, postponing the sale beyond the target price, it could be disastrous.

"But I don't believe you should necessarily sell once a stock has reached its target price. The Berkshire Hathaway annual report has said, `An investor should ordinarily hold a small piece of an outstanding business with the same tenacity that an owner would exhibit if he owned all of that business.' "

One portfolio manager, Susan Byrne of the Westwood Funds, has likened a poor-performing stock to a problem child: It takes away attention that your other children may need. Michael Price has observed that selling a poor-performing stock "clears the mind." Others have noted that if a stock fares poorly, it may be a sign that some people know something that you don't. At the Crabbe and Huson funds, a portfolio manager with a 15 percent loss loses the right to determine whether to hold on to that stock or not. One's self-esteem tends to intrude in the decision-making process.

I had suspected that growth investors would put more emphasis on having a plan in place to determine when you should sell. After all, they want to sell before other growth investors decide to sell. Value investors can sell when an undervalued stock starts rising, reaches its fair value, or even when it climbs above its fair value. My hypothesis was borne out—but only barely.

Art Bonnel: highest (1)
Rudy Carryl: highest (1)
Robert Christensen: average (3)
James Craig: highest (1)
Maureen Cullinane: highest (1)
Hugh Denison: average (3)
Richard Fentin: above average (2)
Mario Gabelli: above average (2)
Peter Hagerman: above average (2)
Richard Huson: above average (2)
Warren Isabelle: highest (1)
Arnold Kaufman: highest (1)
Warren Lammert: highest (1)
William Lippman/Bruce Baughman: NA
Thomas Marsico: highest (1)
Terry Milberger: above average (2)
Gary Pilgrim: above average (2)
Michael Price: above average (2)
Douglas Ramos: highest (1)
Brian Rogers: highest (1)
Eileen Rominger: average (3)
Robert Sanborn: highest (1)
Peter Schliemann: above average (2)
Ralph Seger: average (3)
Sandra Shrewsbury: above average (2)
Richard Strong: above average (2)
Heiko Thieme: above average (2)
Peter Van Dyke: average (3)
Donald Yacktman: below average (4)

Average: 1.857 (somewhat above "above average")
Contrarian: Yacktman (4)
Median growth, 1.727, versus median value, 1.916

Special statistical guides (like...)

Panelist comments:

Sanborn (history): "We look at the whole capitalization of the company being bought, and measure it against the cash flow. Then we adjust the figure by looking at the maintenance capital expenditure, the amount of capital expenditure that we think a company needs to maintain its current level. We also look at capital to revenues, and compare the valuation of a stock with its peers in the industry. But there is no single statistic of overriding importance."

I had in mind guides like price-book ratios, price to sales, book value, and so on. Some panelists emphasized a special statistical guide. Others interpreted the question differently, referring to publications they read.

Art Bonnel: average 3 ("like Value Line")

Rudy Carryl: average 3 ("like charts")

Robert Christensen: below average (4)

James Craig: below average (4)

Maureen Cullinane: lowest (5)

Hugh Denison: NA

Richard Fentin: average (3)

Mario Gabelli: NA

Peter Hagerman: average 3 ("like Value Line")

Richard Huson: average 3 ("like price-sales")

Warren Isabelle: NA

Arnold Kaufman: above average (2)

Warren Lammert: NA

William Lippman/Bruce Baughman: NA

Thomas Marsico: highest (1)

Terry Milberger: NA

Gary Pilgrim: NA

Michael Price: lowest (5)

Douglas Ramos: average (3) ("like low p/e")

Brian Rogers: highest (1) ("like any consistently applied rules")

Eileen Rominger: lowest (5)

Robert Sanborn: highest (1)

Peter Schliemann: lowest (5)

Ralph Seger: above average 3 ("like Standard & Poor's, Value Line")

Sandra Shrewsbury: average 3 ("like a statistical database")

Richard Strong: below average (4)

Heiko Thieme: above average 2 ("like the economy")

Peter Van Dyke: NA

Donald Yacktman: highest (1) ("like internal rate of return")

Responses: 21

Average: 3.14 (slightly below average)

Contrarians: four fives, four ones

Median growth, 3.1, versus median value, 3.33

Experience

Panelist comments:

Isabelle (average): "Experience is important—it tells you when to read between the lines. It tells you when someone is being sincere or when someone is hyping a stock. But while it's helpful, it's not the quintessential factor."

My surmise that there would be little difference here between value and growth investors turned out to be correct. I had an inkling that perhaps growth managers are younger—and therefore less appreciative of experience—but it didn't turn out that way.

Art Bonnel: above average (2)

Rudy Carryl: above average (3)

Robert Christensen: highest (1)

James Craig: highest (1)

Maureen Cullinane: above average (2)

Hugh Denison: above average (2)

Richard Fentin: above average (2)

Mario Gabelli: highest (1)

Peter Hagerman: highest (1)

Richard Huson: above average (2)

Warren Isabelle: average (3)

Arnold Kaufman: NA

Warren Lammert: above average (2)

William Lippman/Bruce Baughman: highest (1)

Thomas Marsico: highest (1)

Terry Milberger: above average (2)

Gary Pilgrim: above average (2)

Michael Price: highest (1)

Douglas Ramos: above average (2)

Brian Rogers: below average (4)

Eileen Rominger: above average (2)

Robert Sanborn: average (3)

Peter Schliemann: above average (2)

Ralph Seger: highest (1)

Sandra Shrewsbury: above average (2)

Richard Strong: above average (2)

Heiko Thieme: above average (2)

Peter Van Dyke: average (3)

Donald Yacktman: below average (4)

Responses: 28
Average: 2.07 ("above average")
Contrarians: Isabelle (5), Rogers and Yacktman (4)
Median growth, 1.91, versus median value, 2.15

Flexibility

Panelist comments:

Isabelle (average): "Flexibility is important because you need to be able to offer a number of interpretations of a possible set of facts. You need the ability to look at more than one potential outcome. Being rigid, you can run into a number of different traps. On the other hand, if you are too flexible, you may invest in too many varieties of stocks, growth and value, and you are likely to hurt yourself. Most investors are skilled only at investing in a few types of stock."

Shrewsbury (below average): "In investing you're always in a very dynamic environment, and you always have to have your antennae out. An example is the changing political conditions after President Clinton's election, and the effect this had on drug company stocks. An investor shouldn't always go with the crowd, but it's important to know what the crowd is doing."

"Flexibility" is a little vague. It can mean a willingness to improvise, to break your own rules, to make exceptions; it can also mean dealing imaginatively with new data—resourcefulness. And it can mean making quick decisions.

Remaining flexible seems contrary to the principle of sticking to your strategy. It suggests occasionally abandoning your strategy—not a bad idea if a strategy seems likely to fall out of favor and remain out of favor for a long time, the way small-cap stocks did in the early 1980s. That's why I suspected that growth investors would appreciate this quality more than value players—and, by a small percentage, they did. Seven of the 11 growth players ranked "flexibility" 1 or 2; only 5 of the 13 value players did so.

Art Bonnel: above average (2)

Rudy Carryl: average (3)

Robert Christensen: average (3)

James Craig: highest (1)

Maureen Cullinane: above average (2)

Hugh Denison: below average (4)

Richard Fentin: below average (4)

Mario Gabelli: average (3)

Peter Hagerman: above average (2)

Richard Huson: above average (2)

Warren Isabelle: average (3)

Arnold Kaufman: NA

Warren Lammert: above average (2)

William Lippman/Bruce Baughman: highest (1)

Thomas Marsico: highest (1)

Terry Milberger: above average (2)

Gary Pilgrim: above average (2)

Michael Price: above average (2)

Douglas Ramos: highest (1)

Brian Rogers: average (3)

Eileen Rominger: below average (4)

Robert Sanborn: above average (2)

Peter Schliemann: average (3)

Ralph Seger: above average (2)

Sandra Shrewsbury: below average (4)

Richard Strong: above average (2)

Heiko Thieme: average (3)

Peter Van Dyke: below average (4)

Donald Yacktman: below average (4)

Responses: 28

Average: 2.607 (somewhat above average)

Contrarians: six voted for "below average"

Median growth, 2.36, versus median value, 2.85

Willingness to be contrarian

Panelist comments:

Shrewsbury (above average): "There's no reason why an investor should always go with the crowd, but it's always important to know what the crowd is doing, and to be able to justify your actions if you go against the behavior of most other investors."

Pilgrim (lowest): "Being a contrarian is not important in my investment approach. It can certainly be in someone else's. Our approach is to recognize those companies where everything is going right, and to watch a consensual approach develop around this investment. I don't have a confrontational approach, investing in companies that the rest of the world wants nothing to do with. I don't want a whole portfolio of out-of-favor stocks. Because if the rest of the world happens to be right, I stand to lose a lot of money."

Contrarian investing would seem to be a staple for value investors, and that's how it turned out in our poll. But some growth investors are crowd-buckers, too, including Richard Strong, James Craig, and Thomas Marsico. And some value investors—like Sanborn—weren't enthusiastic about contrarianism. All of which demonstrates that growth and value investing represent a continuum, that—as Warren Buffett put it—they are joined at the hip.

Art Bonnel: average (3)

Rudy Carryl: below average (4)

Robert Christensen: above average (2)

James Craig: highest (1)

Maureen Cullinane: average (3)

Hugh Denison: above average (2)

Richard Fentin: above average (2)

Mario Gabelli: highest (1)

Peter Hagerman: below average (4)

Richard Huson: highest (1)

Warren Isabelle: highest (1)

Arnold Kaufman: NA

Warren Lammert: above average (2)

William Lippman/Bruce Baughman: highest (1)

Thomas Marsico: highest (1)

Terry Milberger: above average (2)

Gary Pilgrim: lowest (5)

Michael Price: highest (1)

Douglas Ramos: average (3)

Brian Rogers: above average (2)

Eileen Rominger: above average (2)

Robert Sanborn: average (3)

Peter Schliemann: highest (1)

Ralph Seger: average (3)

Sandra Shrewsbury: below average (4)

Richard Strong: above average (2)

Heiko Thieme: highest (1)

Peter Van Dyke: above average (2)

Donald Yacktman: above average (2)

Responses: 28

Average: 2.178 (slightly below "average")

Contrarians: Pilgrim (5)

Median growth, 2.63, versus median value, 1.6

Chapter 11

Good Reasons to Buy a Stock

According to our panelists, capable management is one of the best reasons to buy a company's stock. Another excellent reason: changes for the better, in the company, in the industry, in the economy, or in general.

Beyond those two reasons, growth and value investors take decidedly different paths in deciding which stocks to buy. Growth managers emphasize strong earnings. Value managers like a healthy free-cash flow.

Here are the chief reasons that growth, value, and blend investors give for buying stocks, in descending order of importance (from 1, highest, to 5, lowest.)

Growth investors

Strong earnings growth	1.1
Capable management	1.545
Changes for the better	2.09
Company dominant in field	2.09
New products or services	2.18
Return on equity	2.27
Good industry	2.27
Manager ownership	2.45
Free-cash flow	2.63
High yield/good balance sheet	2.909
Relative strength	2.909
Not followed by big investors	3.183
Low price/earnings ratio	3.27
Something you know that others don't	3.6
Low price-to-book value	3.82

Value investors

Changes for the better	1.75
Capable management	1.75
Manager ownership	1.916
Free-cash flow	2.166
High yield/good balance sheet	2.18
Low price/earnings ratio	2.33
Low price to book value	2.41
Dominant in field	2.66
Return on equity	2.83
Not followed by big investors	2.83
Strong earnings growth	3.25
Good industry	3.33
New products or services	3.33
Something you know that others don't	3.636
Relative strength	4.36

Blend

Dominant in field	2.0
Return on equity	2.0
Low price/earnings ratio	2.22
Strong earnings growth	2.2
Manager ownership	2.4
Changes for the better	2.5
Capable management	2.5
Good industry	2.5
New products or services	2.6
Free-cash flow	2.8
Something you know that others don't	3.0
Not followed by big investors	3.2
High yield/good balance sheet	3.4
Relative strength	3.75
Low price to book value	4.2

Below are the individual questions and a tabulation of the responses. (Michael Price wrote "All reasons listed," without rating any of the reasons to buy.)

What leads you to buy a stock? (Rate from 1, highest, to 5, lowest)

Changes for the better

Panelist comments:

Christensen (highest): "A lot of academic research has shown that surprises on the good side are one of the most important determinants of appreciation in a stock."

Rogers (above average): "I tend to invest in companies that have been under some degree of market stress, hoping that they will gain at some point. Any indication of positive change can augur well for better stock performance. It could be an improvement in a specific company's business fundamentals—it could be anything, depending on the type of business. As a value investor, I believe that my style of investing is basically a well-informed guessing game, and knowing about changes for the better can keep you better informed."

Value investors might not readily buy a stock when the company's prospects are clearly improving because the stock might not be a screaming buy at that point. But in the survey, value investors rated positive changes higher than growth investors did—perhaps because they are assuming that the favorable changes aren't yet reflected in the price.

Art Bonnel: above average (2)

Rudy Carryl: average (3)

Robert Christensen: highest (1)

James Craig: highest (1)

Maureen Cullinane: above average (2)

Hugh Denison: average (3)

Richard Fentin: below average (4)

Mario Gabelli: highest (1)

Peter Hagerman: average (3)

Richard Huson: highest (1)

Warren Isabelle: highest (1)

Arnold Kaufman: NA

Warren Lammert: highest (1)

William Lippman/Bruce Baughman: above average (2)

Thomas Marsico: above average (2)
Terry Milberger: above average (2)

Gary Pilgrim: highest (1)

Douglas Ramos: above average (2)

Brian Rogers: above average (2)

Eileen Rominger: above average (2)

Robert Sanborn: highest (1)

Peter Schliemann: highest (1)

Ralph Seger: above average (2)

Sandra Shrewsbury: average (3)

Richard Strong: average (3)

Heiko Thieme: above average (2)

Peter Van Dyke: above average (2)

Donald Yacktman: below average (4)

Responses: 27

Average: 2.03 (above average)

Contrarians: Fentin, Yacktman (4)

Median growth, 2.09, versus median value, 1.75, versus median blend, 2.5

Low price/earnings ratio

Panelist comments:

Bonnel (above average): "Statistics like this can indicate that a company is undervalued, and maybe you've found something that the Street hasn't discovered yet. One can find some real gems out there. It's like an added bonus. But you must look at these statistics cautiously. By themselves, raw data can be misleading."

Christensen (highest): "With low price/earnings ratios, unpleasant surprises won't hurt the stock so much. So management can take higher risks, because the market is not expecting anything great from this company. Whereas improvements, which are unexpected, can significantly boost a stock's performance. Conversely, with a high p/e stock, the market doesn't reward it very much because the market already had high expectations for the company."

Isabelle (average): "It's only a very rough gauge. A lot of companies have write-offs, so you don't get a true picture of the earnings. Also, a company may be in a transition, so you can get a downright misleading picture."

This question was intended to separate the value players from the growth. Did it? Yes, but there was a scary moment—when it became clear that such value players as Fentin, Gabelli, and Huson considered a low price/earnings ratio "below average" in importance.

Art Bonnel: above average (2)

Rudy Carryl: average (3)

Robert Christensen: highest (1)

James Craig: below average (4)

Maureen Cullinane: below average (4)

Hugh Denison: highest (1)

Richard Fentin: below average (4)

Mario Gabelli: below average (4)

Peter Hagerman:below average (4)

Richard Huson: below average (4)

Warren Isabelle: average (3)

Arnold Kaufman: highest (1)

Warren Lammert: highest (1) ("relative to growth")

William Lippman/Bruce Baughman: above average (2)

Thomas Marsico: average (3)

Terry Milberger: average (3)

Gary Pilgrim: lowest (5)

Douglas Ramos: highest (1)

Brian Rogers: highest (1)

Eileen Rominger: above average (2)

Robert Sanborn: above average (2)

Peter Schliemann: average (3)

Ralph Seger: above average (2)

Sandra Shrewsbury: below average (4)

Richard Strong: below average (4)

Heiko Thieme: above average (2)

Peter Van Dyke: average (3)

Donald Yacktman: above average (2)

Responses: 28

Average: 2.68 (between "average" and "above average")

Contrarians: 8 with (4), 1 with (5), 7 with (1)—an unusually
   sharp divergence

Median growth, 3.27, versus median value, 2.33

Low price-to-book value

Panelist comments:

Isabelle (lowest): "It depends on the kinds of stock. It's irrelevent
with service and consumer-oriented stocks. It's more relevant with
large, mature industries with nondepreciating, fixed assets. I'm more
interested in high returns on total invested capital."

Sanborn (average): "Because of the different ways people calculate
it, it's become almost a meaningless concept."

Yacktman (below average): "The value of a business isn't determined by its balance sheet but by its cash-generating ability, which
is largely determined by the type of assets and the use to which these
assets are put. The internal rate of return is important if you're concerned about what's happening in the business, what the company
does with its money. The internal rate of return is more accurate in
telling how strong a company is."

Again, the value players were expected to carry the flag here. And
they did—despite defections by Isabelle, Ramos, and Rominger. And
growth players behaved themselves—except for Bonnel.

Art Bonnel: highest (1)

Rudy Carryl: below average (4)

Robert Christensen: highest (1)

James Craig: below average (4)

Maureen Cullinane: below average (4)

Hugh Denison: highest (1)

Richard Fentin: above average (2)

Mario Gabelli: average (3)

Peter Hagerman: below average (4)

Richard Huson: above average (2)

Warren Isabelle: lowest (5)

Arnold Kaufman: lowest (5)

Warren Lammert: average (3)

William Lippman/Bruce Baughman: highest (1)

Thomas Marsico: lowest (5)

Terry Milberger: lowest (5)

Gary Pilgrim: lowest (5)

Douglas Ramos: below average (4)

Brian Rogers: highest (1)

Eileen Rominger: below average (4)

Robert Sanborn: average (3) change

Peter Schliemann: above average (2)

Ralph Seger: lowest (5)

Sandra Shrewsbury: below average (4)

Richard Strong: below average (4)

Heiko Thieme: average (3)

Peter Van Dyke: average (3)

Donald Yacktman: below average (4)

Responses: 28

Average: 3.28 (somewhat below average)

Contrarians: five with (5), six with (1)—again, an unusual divergence.

Median growth, 3.82, versus median value, 2.41

Strong earnings growth

Panelist comments:

Bonnel (highest): "I like good, solid earnings growth over a number of years. "

Isabelle (lowest): "Everyone likes strong earnings growth. But some of my best investments were made when there was no earnings growth. I'm looking to find a company selling at a low price, when it's not doing what people want, when it has a low earnings-growth rate. Unless you find that rare, rare instance when no one's discovered a stock's strong earnings growth yet."

Yacktman (below average): "If you look just at strong earnings growth, you get to the wrong place. Many companies are cyclical: They perform well, decline, perform well, and so on. If you just look at earnings growth, a decline may appear to have been translated into growth, but this is deceptive. It's merely part of a cycle. You need a long-term approach."

Now it should be the growth players' turn, and they were true to form. Earnings growth is clearly their Holy Grail. But, oddly, it was also the Holy Grail for one value player, Sanborn. But he's generally regarded as a value/growth investor.

Art Bonnel: highest (1)
Rudy Carryl: highest (1)
Robert Christensen: average (3)
James Craig: highest (1)
Maureen Cullinane: highest (1)
Hugh Denison: average (3)
Richard Fentin: below average (4)
Mario Gabelli: average (3)
Peter Hagerman: highest (1)
Richard Huson: below average (4)
Warren Isabelle: lowest (5)
Arnold Kaufman: above average (2)

Warren Lammert: average (3)

William Lippman/Bruce Baughman: average (3)

Thomas Marsico: above average (2)

Terry Milberger: highest (1)

Gary Pilgrim: highest (1)

Douglas Ramos: above average (2)

Brian Rogers: average (3)

Eilen Rominger: average (3)

Robert Sanborn: highest (1)

Peter Schliemann: below average (4)

Ralph Seger: highest (1)

Sandra Shrewsbury: highest (1)

Richard Strong: highest (1)

Heiko Thieme: above average (2)

Peter Van Dyke: highest (1)

Donald Yacktman: below average (4)

Responses: 28

Average: 2.25 (somewhat below "above average")

Contrarian: Isabelle (5)

Median growth, 1.1, versus median value, 3.25

Free-cash flow

Panelists' comments:

Bonnel (above average): "I don't look at free-cash flow that closely. Cash flow is more important in identifying a bargain where a company is a potential takeover candidate. But that's not the kind of investment I'm interested in."

Pilgrim (lowest): "I don't feel it's a necessary tool for us. We focus on earnings per share and sales momentum. Free-cash flow doesn't necessarily show corporate success. In many cases, a lack of free-cash flow is actually a good sign because it could show that companies are reinvesting their money, borrowing to expand the company, or even lending out money to bring more in later. A free-cash flow could show that a company isn't adequately exploiting the opportunities."

Free-cash flow is apparently a clue, to value investors, that a company has a good prognosis, despite a weak pulse.

Art Bonnel: above average (2)

Rudy Carryl: below average (4)

Robert Christensen: below average (4)

James Craig: above average (2)

Maureen Cullinane: below average (4)

Hugh Denison: highest (1)

Richard Fentin: average (3)

Mario Gabelli: highest (1)

Peter Hagerman: below average (4)

Richard Huson: highest (1)

Warren Isabelle: highest (1)

Arnold Kaufman: below average (4)

Warren Lammert: above average (2)

William Lippman/Bruce Baughman: above average (2)

Thomas Marsico: average (3)

Terry Milberger: average (3)

Gary Pilgrim: lowest (5)

Douglas Ramos: average (3)

Brian Rogers: highest (1)

Eileen Rominger: highest (1)

Robert Sanborn: lowest (5)

Peter Schliemann: average (3)

Ralph Seger: above average (2)

Sandra Shrewsbury: above average (2)

Richard Strong: highest (1)

Heiko Thieme: above average (2)
Peter Van Dyke: average (3)
Donald Yacktman: highest (1)

Responses: 28
Average: 2.50 (between "average" and "above average")
Contrarians: 8 with (1), 2 with (5).
Median growth, 2.63, versus median value, 2.166

Return on equity

Panelist comments:

Isabelle (lowest): "I like to buy before a company has a good return on equity, when I feel it will rise in the future. I buy stock when I feel the company's management can easily be improved, or the existing capital put to more efficient use."

This is an especially appropriate guide for growth investors.

Art Bonnel: highest (1)
Rudy Carryl: average (3)
Robert Christensen: average (3)
James Craig: above average (2)
Maureen Cullinane: above average (2)
Hugh Denison: average (3)
Richard Fentin: above average (2)
Mario Gabelli: below average (4)
Peter Hagerman: highest (1)
Richard Huson: average (3)
Warren Isabelle: lowest (5)
Arnold Kaufman: NA
Warren Lammert: above average (2)
William Lippman/Bruce Baughman: above average (2)

Thomas Marsico: average (3)

Terry Milberger: average (3)

Gary Pilgrim: average (3)

Douglas Ramos: above average (2)

Brian Rogers: average (3)

Eileen Rominger: highest (1)

Robert Sanborn: above average (2)

Peter Schliemann: below average (4)

Ralph Seger: highest (1)

Sandra Shrewsbury: average (3)

Richard Strong: highest (1)

Heiko Thieme: above average (2)

Peter Van Dyke: below average (4)

Donald Yacktman: above average (2)

Responses: 27

Average: 2.48 (between "average" and "above average")

Contrarian: Isabelle (5)

Median growth, 2.27, versus median value, 2.833

Capable management

Panelist comments:

Christensen (average): "With better management, there's more likelihood of positive changes than with a management committed to maintaining the status quo."

Rogers (above average): "There are a couple of different schools of thought about this. The assessment of a management group's being capable is very subjective. But from a long-term standpoint, you don't want to invest with a bunch of bozos."

No difference in sentiment between value and growth investors was predicted. But there was slightly more emphasis given to this factor by growth players—perhaps because some value investors believe that a company itself will right itself, not necessarily the managers.

Art Bonnel: highest (1)

Rudy Carryl: above average (2)

Robert Christensen: average (3)

James Craig: highest (1)

Maureen Cullinane: above average (2)

Hugh Denison: highest (1)

Richard Fentin: average (3)

Mario Gabelli: highest (1)

Peter Hagerman: average (3)

Richard Huson: average (3)

Warren Isabelle: highest (1)

Arnold Kaufman: highest (1)

Warren Lammert: highest (1)

William Lippman/Bruce Baughman: highest (1)

Thomas Marsico: highest (1)

Terry Milberger: highest (1)

Gary Pilgrim: average (3)

Douglas Ramos: above average (2)

Brian Rogers: above average (2)

Eileen Rominger: highest (1)

Robert Sanborn: highest (1)

Peter Schliemann: above average (2)

Ralph Seger: highest (1)

Sandra Shrewsbury: highest (1)

Richard Strong: highest (1)

Heiko Thieme: above average (2)

Peter Van Dyke: above average (2)

Donald Yacktman: above average (2)

Responses: 28

Average: 1.65

Contrarians: Three panelists gave this only an average rating

Median growth, 1.545, versus median value, 1.75

Good industry

Panelists' comments:

Isabelle (lowest): "You want to make sure that the industry isn't going away. But I'm not worried about cylical downturns in an industry's performance. I'm also not averse to buying a strong firm in an overall weak industry. I've bought several steel companies despite the unfavorable climate for American steel in recent years."

Pilgrim (below average): "We don't evaluate industries. We think it's more important to understand how companies are going. We are just looking for companies that are exploiting opportunities. Many of the small firms we specialize in don't actually belong to recognized industries as such, whereas in older, larger companies these are often affected by industry trends—for example, car-manufacturing companies. In the smaller arena, the industry is often an arbitrary classification."

Value investors may prefer stocks in cyclical industries on the downturn, or just in depressed industries, rather than growing industries, which may be everyone's favorites and therefore overpriced.

Art Bonnel: above average (2)

Rudy Carryl: above average (2)

Robert Christensen: below average (4)

James Craig: average (3)

Maureen Cullinane: above average (2)

Hugh Denison: below average (4)

Richard Fentin: above average (2)

Mario Gabelli: above average (2)

Peter Hagerman: average (3)

Richard Huson: below average (4)

Warren Isabelle: lowest (5)

Arnold Kaufman: above average (2)

Warren Lammert: above average (2)

William Lippman/Bruce Baughman: average (3)

Thomas Marsico: highest (1)

Terry Milberger: above average (2)

Gary Pilgrim: below average (4)

Douglas Ramos: average (3)

Brian Rogers: average (3)

Eileen Rominger: average (3)

Robert Sanborn: below average (4)

Peter Schliemann: average (3)

Ralph Seger: above average (2)

Sandra Shrewsbury: above average (2)

Richard Strong: highest (1)

Heiko Thieme: below average (4)

Peter Van Dyke: above average (2)

Donald Yacktman: highest (1)

Responses: 26

Average: 2.88 (somewhat above "average")

Contrarians: 9 with (1), 1 with (5)

Median growth, 2.27, versus median value, 3.33

Dominant in field

Panelists' comments:

Rogers (below average): "That's less important than the valuation. I would rather buy a company with a third market position if it had a good price than the leading market-position company if the price were wrong. It gets back to my basic belief that the price is the leading determinant of the success of an investment."

Isabelle (lowest): "It's always nice to have the situation line up that way, but what you want is a company with a trend in the right direction. I look for companies with adventurous, fresh management. That's when you get the investment leverage you need. Sometimes a dominant company really has no place to go but down."

The value players, logically, were somewhat less enthusiastic about companies dominant in their fields, presumably because their prices may also be higher than companies not dominant in their fields.

Art Bonnel: highest (1)

Rudy Carryl: highest (1)

Robert Christensen: average (3)

James Craig: average (3)

Maureen Cullinane: above average (2)

Hugh Denison: average (3)

Richard Fentin: average (3)

Mario Gabelli: highest (1)

Peter Hagerman: average (3)

Richard Huson: average (3)

Warren Isabelle: lowest (5)

Arnold Kaufman: NA

Warren Lammert: above average (2)

William Lippman/Bruce Baughman: average (3)

Thomas Marsico: highest (1)

Terry Milberger: above average (2)

Gary Pilgrim: below average (4)

Douglas Ramos: average (3)

Brian Rogers: below average (4)

Eileen Rominger: highest (1)

Robert Sanborn: highest (1)

Peter Schliemann: above average (2)

Ralph Seger: above average (2)

Sandra Shrewsbury: above average (2)

Richard Strong: highest (1)

Heiko Thieme: below average (4)

Peter Van Dyke: above average (2)

Donald Yacktman: highest (1)

Responses: 26

Average: 2.42

Contrarians: 9 with (1), 3 with (4)

Median growth, 2.091, versus median value, 2.666

Manager ownership

Panelist comments:

Sanborn (highest): "If a company is management-owned, Oakmark is more likely to buy it. We view management-owned companies as more likely to grow."

Isabelle (average): "I like to see people who are at risk, like I am. But I'll buy companies where management doesn't have any ownership because it can change."

Pilgrim (lowest): "In small companies, manager ownership is marginal information that is only of peripheral value. In the small- and emerging-growth categories, managers typically start off owning quite a lot and then routinely dispose of it when the company becomes successful. Insider selling in these situatons is routine. It is only in larger, more mature companies that issues of manager ownership become a little more meaningful."

One might have expected this reason for buying to be high-ranked by growth, value, and blend investors. But it emerged only somewhat above average. Value players, not surprisingly, emphasized manager ownership more than growth players.

Art Bonnel: highest (1)

Rudy Carryl: above average (2)

Robert Christensen: average (3)

James Craig: above average (2)

Maureen Cullinane: average (3)

Hugh Denison: highest (1)

Richard Fentin: average (3)

Mario Gabelli: above average (2)

Peter Hagerman: average (3)

Richard Huson: average (3)

Warren Isabelle: average (1)

Arnold Kaufman: average (3)

Warren Lammert: above average (2)

William Lippman/Bruce Baughman: highest (1)

Thomas Marsico: above average (2)

Terry Milberger: above average (2)

Gary Pilgrim: lowest (5)

Douglas Ramos: average (3)

Brian Rogers: average (3)

Eileen Rominger: highest (1)

Robert Sanborn: highest (1)

Peter Schliemann: highest (1)

Ralph Seger: above average (2)

Sandra Shrewsbury: above average (2)

Richard Strong: highest (1)

Heiko Thieme: below average (4)

Peter Van Dyke: average (3)

Donald Yacktman: above average (2)

Responses: 28

Average: 2.21 (almost "above average")

Contrarians: Pilgrim (5)

Median growth, 2.45, versus median value, 1.916

New products or services

Panelist comments:

Rogers (below average): "New products may or may not be good. If you're Quaker Oats and you introduce one new product every three or four years, your old products will still be doing well. Exxon essentially hasn't had a new product in 70 years. To me, valuation is more important than new products."

Yacktman (below average): "If I had a choice between high asset returns and great unit growth in a company, I would choose the high asset returns. It's not of paramount importance that a company is marketing new products and services as long as they are using their assets smartly."

The question should have been phrased: "promising new products or services." Growth managers clearly were energized by this possibility. Value players were markedly less enthusiastic. Perhaps growth players regard new products and services from growing companies as more likely to succeed than new products and services from depressed companies. Or new products and services may be more important to the success of smaller, growing companies than larger, stable companies.

Art Bonnel: highest (1)

Rudy Carryl: highest (1)

Robert Christensen: below average (4)

James Craig: highest (1)

Maureen Cullinane: above average (2)

Hugh Denison: below average (4)

Richard Fentin: below average (4)

Mario Gabelli: average (3)

Peter Hagerman: average (3)

Richard Huson: above average (2)

Warren Isabelle: average (3)

Arnold Kaufman: above average (2)

Warren Lammert: above average (2)

William Lippman/Bruce Baughman: below average (4)

Thomas Marsico: average (3)

Terry Milberger: above average (2)

Gary Pilgrim: above average (2)

Douglas Ramos: below average (4)

Brian Rogers: below average (4)

Eileen Rominger: below average (4)

Robert Sanborn: highest (1)

Peter Schliemann: average (3)

Ralph Seger: average (3)

Sandra Shrewsbury: average (3)

Richard Strong: above average (2)

Heiko Thieme: below average (4)

Peter Van Dyke: above average (2)

Donald Yacktman: below average (4)

Responses: 28

Average: 2.75

Contrarians: 8 with (4)

Median growth, 2.182, versus median value, 3.33

High yield/good balance sheet

Panelist comments:

Isabelle (lowest): "I've bought stock with no debt — and stock with 100 percent leverage. If I buy a company in debt, I'm looking for compensating factors like future potential."

Pilgrim (lowest): "High dividends are irrelevant to a growth stock. These companies don't pay dividends. We want these companies to reinvest their yields. We do care about a good balance sheet. It's a good character reference. We don't like companies that have low margins and lots of debt."

Yacktman (lowest): "It implies that management is not being aggressive enough. Imagine two companies that both earn 15 percent returns. One pays 60 percent of that out in dividends, the other holds it all back, using it to buy back shares, to invest, and so on. Money given back to shareholders in the form of dividends will be taxed, so it isn't being used as effectively as it would if it had paid interest on loans, for example. If I had a business, I'd rather it were a company that had a single A rating rather than a triple A."

That value investors weren't more impressed by high dividends and a good balance sheet was surprising. Perhaps it is a tool used by less sophisticated value investors.

Art Bonnel: highest (1)

Rudy Carryl: average (3)

Robert Christensen: average (3)

James Craig: below average (4)

Maureen Cullinane: average (3)

Hugh Denison: average (3)

Richard Fentin: above average (2)

Mario Gabelli: average (3)

Peter Hagerman: above average (2)

Richard Huson: average (3)

Warren Isabelle: lowest (5)

Arnold Kaufman: average (3)

Warren Lammert: lowest (5)

William Lippman/Bruce Baughman: (two separate items—NA)

Thomas Marsico: average (3)

Terry Milberger: average (3)

Gary Pilgrim: lowest (5)

Douglas Ramos: average (3)

Brian Rogers: highest (1)

Eileen Rominger: below average (4)

Robert Sanborn: highest (1)

Peter Schliemann: average (3)

Ralph Seger: above average (2) (only "good balance sheet")

Sandra Shrewsbury: average (3)

Richard Strong: average (3)

Heiko Thieme: above average (2)

Peter Van Dyke: average (3)

Donald Yacktman: below average (4)

Responses: 28

Average: 2.857

Contrarians: Isabelle, Lammert, Pilgrim (5)

Median growth, 2.909, versus. median value, 2.18

Not followed by big investors

Panelist comments:

Shrewsbury (below average): "If a stock has a big backing, it's seen as safer for small investors. They can sell without its having a catastrophic effect on the price of the stock. If the fundamentals are strong, yet for some reason the big investors aren't buying, it could be a great discovery: The stock might be considerably undervalued. Neglected stocks do often perform better. But it's the fundamentals of the company that make my decision, not who else owns the stock."

Yacktman (lowest): "Should I make decisions based on what other large-scale investors are doing? The answer is no. One should make decisions standing on one's own two feet. There is a very expensive price paid for consensus."

This reason for buying a stock might appeal especially to value investors, who search for flowers blooming unseen. Although some studies have apparently confirmed the wisdom of investing in underfollowed stocks, the panelists weren't especially impressed— particularly the growth investors. Perhaps growth investors want their stocks to be discovered sooner rather than later. (In Yacktman's case, and perhaps others, the question seems to have been misinterpreted; its meaning could have been clearer.)

Art Bonnel: average (3)
Rudy Carryl: below average (4)
Robert Christensen: lowest (5)
James Craig: below average (4)
Maureen Cullinane: average (3)
Hugh Denison: above average (2)
Richard Fentin: below average (4)
Mario Gabelli: above average (2)
Peter Hagerman: average (3)
Richard Huson: average (3)
Warren Isabelle: above average (2)
Arnold Kaufman: average (3)
Warren Lammert: average (2)
William Lippman/Bruce Baughman: above average (2)
Thomas Marsico: above average (2)
Terry Milberger: average (3)
Gary Pilgrim: lowest (5)
Douglas Ramos: average (3)
Brian Rogers: below average (4)
Eileen Rominger: average (3)
Robert Sanborn: average (3)
Peter Schliemann: highest (1)
Ralph Seger: average (3)
Sandra Shrewsbury: below average (4)
Richard Strong: average (3)
Heiko Thieme: average (3)
Peter Van Dyke: highest (1)
Donald Yacktman: lowest (5)

Responses: 28

Average: 3.03 (average)

Contrarians: Christensen, Pilgrim, Yacktman (5); Schlieman, Van Dyke (1)

Median growth, 3.182, versus median value, 2.83

Relative strength

Panelist comments:

Isabelle (lowest): "I'm interested in a company as a company. I don't care what its price is relative to other prices. That's a problem too many people have. But I probably wouldn't buy into a company if I felt the price was likely to remain weak more than just a short time."

Pilgrim (average): "We think it's more important to follow the fundamental trends of our companies. Relative strength can be a very misleading short-term indicator. Bad price behavior is kind of an orange light rather than a red light. It is a warning that things may be wrong, but of itself it is not enough to have a decisive influence on whether to sell a stock."

This reason to buy a stock should appeal to growth investors: The stock is beginning to move. But apparently most growth investors think it may be too late to buy a stock whose price is already rising. Value players, of course, have little use for this signal.

Art Bonnel: above average (2)

Rudy Carryl: above average (2)

Robert Christensen: average (3)

James Craig: lowest (5)

Maureen Cullinane: above average (2)

Hugh Denison: below average (4)

Richard Fentin: below average (4)

Mario Gabelli: below average (4)

Peter Hagerman: below average (4)

Richard Huson: lowest (5)

Warren Isabelle: lowest (5)

Arnold Kaufman: NA

Warren Lammert: below average (4)

William Lippman/Bruce Baughman: lowest (5)

Thomas Marsico: average (3)

Terry Milberger: above average (2)

Gary Pilgrim: average (3)

Douglas Ramos: lowest (5)

Brian Rogers: below average (4)

Eileen Rominger: lowest (5)

Robert Sanborn: highest (1)

Peter Schliemann: average (3)

Ralph Seger: lowest (5)

Sandra Shrewsbury: average (3)

Richard Strong: average (3)

Heiko Thieme: below average (4)

Peter Van Dyke: average (3)

Donald Yacktman: lowest (5)

Responses: 28

Average: 3.5 (between "below average" and "average")

Contrarian: Sanborn (1)

Median growth, 2.909, versus median value, 4.36, versus median blend 3.75

Something you know that others don't

Panelist comments:

Isabelle (highest): "It's a game of information: Who has the best knowledge, and who interprets it best. Any information I have that others don't might give me an edge in making decisions. A good example is Avondale Industies, a shipyard that most people thought was sinking into bankruptcy. We found the information that there was quite a bit of activity with the company. We bought into the stock at $1 and sold at $7."

This question scared some panelists, who interpreted it to mean information they shouldn't ethically have—"inside" information. It was intended to mean only that an investor knew that (say) a product's popularity was waning, thanks to (say) information from competitors.

Art Bonnel: average (3)

Rudy Carryl: lowest (5)

Robert Christensen: average (3)

James Craig: NA

Maureen Cullinane: average (3)

Hugh Denison: below average (4)

Richard Fentin: lowest (5)

Mario Gabelli: below average (4)

Peter Hagerman: below average (4)

Richard Huson: below average (4)

Warren Isabelle: highest (1)

Arnold Kaufman: NA

Warren Lammert: above average (2)

William Lippman/Bruce Baughman: lowest (5)

Thomas Marsico: above average (2)

Terry Milberger: average (3)

Gary Pilgrim: lowest (5)

Douglas Ramos: lowest (5)

Brian Rogers: average (3)

Eileen Rominger: NA

Robert Sanborn: average (3)

Peter Schliemann: average (3)

Ralph Seger: above average (2)

Sandra Shrewsbury: lowest (5)
Richard Strong: average (3)
Heiko Thieme: lowest (5)
Peter Van Dyke: average (3)
Donald Yacktman: average (3)

Responses: 25
Average: 3.52
Contrarians: Isabelle (1)
Median growth, 3.6, versus median value 3.63

Other reasons the panelists gave to buy a stock:

Richard Fentin: Price/sales ratio: above average (2)
Richard Huson: Catalyst to change investors attitudes: highest (1)
Eileen Rominger: Return on invested capital: highest (1)
Ralph Seger: Interest coverage: highest (1)
Ralph Seger: Less than historical average p/e ratio: highest (1)
Douglas Ramos: Low dividend payout: average (3)

Chapter 12

How Long Should You Own the Typical Stock?

O ur panelists generally hold individual stocks for just two or three years. That confirms the conventional wisdom that one should hold a stock for about three years to give it a fair chance to prove itself.

The most aggressive, growth-oriented investors—like Richard Strong—own stocks for less than a year. Dyed-in-the-wool value-oriented investors, like Mario Gabelli, hold stocks for four or five years.

In our poll, growth investors, as expected, kept their stocks for a shorter period of time (less than two-three years) than value investors (more than two-three years). The average of the growth investors was dragged down by Strong and Bonnel, but it was raised by Seger and Van Dyke.

As mentioned, value investors may be forced to wait longer for a depressed stock to rebound than growth investors must wait before a high-flier starts turning into a low-flier.

How long do you normally hold onto a stock?

Art Bonnel: less than 1 year

Rudy Carryl: 2–3 years

Robert Christensen: 2–3 years

James Craig: 1 year

Maureen Cullinane: 1 year

Hugh Denison: 2–3 years

Richard Fentin: 2–3 years

Mario Gabelli: 4–5 years

Peter Hagerman: 2–3 years

Richard Huson: 1 year

Warren Isabelle: 2–3 years

Arnold Kaufman: 2–3 years

Warren Lammert: 1 year

William Lippman/Bruce Baughman: 2-3 years

Thomas Marsico: 1 year

Terry Milberger: 2–3 years

Gary Pilgrim: 2–3 years

Michael Price: NA

Douglas Ramos: 2–3 years

Brian Rogers: 2–3 years

Eileen Rominger: 2–3 years

Robert Sanborn: 4–5 years

Peter Schliemann: 4–5 years

Ralph Seger: longer than 5 years

Sandra Shrewsbury: 2–3 years

Richard Strong: less than a year

Heiko Thieme: 2–3 years ("I also trade aggressively")

Peter Van Dyke: 4–5 years

Donald Yacktman: 4–5 years

Responses: 29

Average: 2–3 years

Median: 2–3 years

Contrarians: Seger (over 5 years), Bonnel and Strong (less than 1 year)

Median growth (less than 2–3 years) versus median value (longer than 2–3 years)

Chapter 13

When to Sell a Stock

S elling, some money managers claim, is the hardest part of investing. In fact, our 29 panelists ranked "selling too soon" and "selling too late" as two of the three most common mistakes they make, the third being buying too soon. (More on this in Chapter 14.)

If you sell too soon, you lose much of the stock's future appreciation. Selling too late means, of course, that the stock's price has already begun plunging. Bernard Baruch, a noted investor and an adviser to Presidents, once said that he *always* sold too soon—meaning that he played it safe. Many of today's managers I talk to say the same thing. (Many also tell me that they never heard of Bernard Baruch.)

I had thought that growth managers would be quicker on the trigger. Growing companies can become valuable—or not so valuable—rather speedily. Undervalued stocks can take a long time to become growth stocks. This suggests that growth managers would be more concerned with selling—and would stress reasons to sell, and rank them higher. They would also be less attached to their stocks.

Growth managers did emphasize selling "when the fundamentals decline" (the earnings falter, for example, or the price/earnings ratio becomes unusually high) and "when the price falls significantly." They do seem quicker on the trigger. Perhaps they are also inclined to sell when the price falls because they are less knowledgeable about their stocks; perhaps value investors know their companies so well that they can dismiss unusual movements.

Value managers emphasized selling when a stock reaches their target price. A conservative stance dictates that they take their money and run before a stock becomes overpriced.

Here, according to the panelists, are the chief reasons to sell a stock, followed by the average of ballots from growth managers and value managers (1 is highest, 5 is lowest):

1. When a key reason for buying disappears (1.82)—growth, 1.818; value, 1.75.
2. When the fundamentals decline (1.32)—growth, 1.091; value, 1.58.
3. When the stock reaches your target price (2.17)—growth, 3.09; value, 1.5.
4. When there's a better investment (2.88)—growth, 3.2; value, 2.92.
5. When you don't understand a stock's movements (3.33)—growth, 3.72; value, 3.
6. When the price falls significantly (3.39)—growth, 3.18; value, 3.58.

Details follow of how the panelists voted on the question, When would you sell a stock?

When a key reason for buying vanishes

Panelist comments:

Sanborn (lowest): "The principal concern is the price, not that a key reason for buying vanishes. We prefer to buy when the price is 60 percent of the underlying value of the company and sell when the price reaches 90 percent of the underlying value. Even so, this is a case-by-case issue."

Pilgrim (average): "Normally I will sell if the buy formula begins to deteriorate." [The buy formula is part of a well-defined strategy, centering on companies with a growth rate higher than 20 percent, a rate that is accelerating, and where earnings estimates are going up.] "If a company starts to slow down from those rates, it is normally sold."

Yacktman (average): "It's a matter of degree. Sometimes something so dramatic happens that a business ceases to be a good investment. But most of the time, businesses don't change that much. If a company owns a high percentage of its market, it's hard for competitors to take that from them. It's easier for that company to screw up and lose its market share through its own poor judgment.

Consequentially, a key reason for buying disappears pretty infrequently. Basically, it happens only when a company self-destructs."

I had expected that this guideline would elicit a high rating from everyone, but I underestimated the independent thinking of money managers.

Art Bonnel: highest (1)

Rudy Carryl: highest (1)

Robert Christensen: highest (1)

James Craig: highest (1)

Maureen Cullinane: highest (1)

Hugh Denison: above average (2)

Richard Fentin: above average (2)

Mario Gabelli: above average (2)

Peter Hagerman: average (3)

Richard Huson: highest (1)

Warren Isabelle: highest (1)

Arnold Kaufman: average (3)

Warren Lammert: highest (1)

William Lippman/Bruce Baughman: highest (1)

Thomas Marsico: highest (1)

Terry Milberger: highest (1)

Gary Pilgrim: average (3)

Michael Price: NA

Douglas Ramos: highest (1)

Brian Rogers: average (3)

Eileen Rominger: highest (1)

Robert Sanborn: lowest (5)

Peter Schliemann: highest (1)

Ralph Seger: below average (4)

Sandra Shrewsbury: highest (1)

Richard Strong: highest (1)

Heiko Thieme: above average (2)

Peter Van Dyke: average (3)

Donald Yacktman: average (3)

Responses: 28

Average: 1.82 (slightly higher than "above average")

Contrarians: Sanborn (5), Seger (4)

Median growth, 1.818, versus median value, 1.75

When the fundamentals decline

Growth investors would be expected to pay more attention to this item, being focused more on the short-term, and they did. But value investors get discouraged, too. Ten out of 11 growth managers rated a decline in fundamentals a 1; 7 out of 12 value investors did so as well.

Art Bonnel: highest (1)

Rudy Carryl: highest (1)

Robert Christensen: highest (1)

James Craig: highest (1)

Maureen Cullinane: highest (1)

Hugh Denison: highest (1)

Richard Fentin: below average (4)

Mario Gabelli: highest (1)

Peter Hagerman: highest (1)

Richard Huson: average (3)

Warren Isabelle: highest (1)

Arnold Kaufman: highest (1)

Warren Lammert: highest (1)

William Lippman/Bruce Baughman: highest (1)

Thomas Marsico: highest (1)

Terry Milberger: highest (1)

Gary Pilgrim: highest (1)

Michael Price: NA

Douglas Ramos: highest (1)

Brian Rogers: above average (2)

Eileen Rominger: highest (1)

Robert Sanborn: highest (1)

Peter Schliemann: above average (2)

Ralph Seger: highest (1)

Sandra Shrewsbury: highest (1)

Richard Strong: highest (1)

Heiko Thieme: above average (2)

Peter Van Dyke: highest (1)

Donald Yacktman: above average (2)

Responses: 28

Average: 1.32 (close to highest)

Contrarian: Fentin (4)

Median growth, 1.091, versus median value, 1.58

When it reaches your target price

Panelist comments:

Bonnel (below average): "I don't set target prices. I might say to myself, `I think the stock could go to this level,' but I believe in letting stocks go. There's the old theory that a pendulum swings further in one direction than you think it will. I generally sell when the fundamentals of the business start to break down or I see management liquidating their shares.

"Besides, sometimes a stock goes up very high, then there's a short squeeze, driving the price up by 40 percent or more. During a short squeeze, the highest profits can be made."

Pilgrim (lowest): "We don't have target prices. We don't think the proper price for a stock can be properly determined. The setting of a target price can only be normative. The price on any given day is the right price. We sell when we feel the fundamentals are no longer strong rather than when some normative target has been reached."

Sanborn (highest): "We'll migrate to a stock with higher expected returns."

Shrewsbury (average): "The target price is rather an artificial number. It's not a perfect number. I don't sit around to figure out the target price of many of my stocks. There's no correct target price. It's a largely psychological construct."

A remarkable disparity. Apparently it confirms how conservative and careful value players are. Value investors seem to emphasize this reason to sell a stock, perhaps because it's easier to determine when an undervalued stock has become properly valued than when a growth stock has reached its proper value. A growth stock's fundamentals may be more erratic and unpredictable, and a price set in advance to sell the stock may keep changing.

Art Bonnel: below average (4)
Rudy Carryl: average (3)
Robert Christensen: above average (2)
James Craig: highest (1)
Maureen Cullinane: above average (2)
Hugh Denison: above average (2)
Richard Fentin: highest (1)
Mario Gabelli: highest (1)
Peter Hagerman: below average (4)
Richard Huson: above average (2)
Warren Isabelle: highest (1)
Arnold Kaufman: highest (1)
Warren Lammert: highest (1)
William Lippman/Bruce Baughman: highest (1)
Thomas Marsico: above average (2)
Terry Milberger: above average (2)
Gary Pilgrim: lowest (5)
Michael Price: highest (1)

Douglas Ramos: highest (1)
Brian Rogers: above average (2)
Eileen Rominger: highest (1)
Robert Sanborn: highest (1)
Peter Schliemann: average (3)
Ralph Seger: lowest (5)
Sandra Shrewsbury: average (3)
Richard Strong: above average (2)
Heiko Thieme: average (3)
Peter Van Dyke: below average (4)
Donald Yacktman: above average (2)

Responses: 29
Average: 2.17 (significantly above average)
Contrarians: Craig, Fentin, Gabelli, Isabelle, Kaufman, Lammert, Lippman/Baughman, Price, Ramos, Rominger (1); Pilgrim (5)
Median growth, 3.09, versus median value, 1.5

Another reason to sell was cited by Seger: When the p/e ratio, based on estimated earnings per share 12 months out, is greater than historic average high p/e ratio: highest (1).

When there's a better investment

Panelist comments:

Sanborn (above average): "This is a competitive business, and it's important if a competitive investment becomes available."

Author Comment: Not much difference between growth and value investors here.

Art Bonnel: above average (2)
Rudy Carryl: below average (4)
Robert Christensen: above average (2)
James Craig: NA

Maureen Cullinane: above average (2)

Hugh Denison: average (3)

Richard Fentin: average (3)

Mario Gabelli: average (3)

Peter Hagerman: above average (2)

Richard Huson: average (3)

Warren Isabelle: lowest (5)

Arnold Kaufman: highest (1)

Warren Lammert: average (3)

William Lippman/Bruce Baughman: below average (4)

Thomas Marsico: average (3)

Terry Milberger: above average (2)

Gary Pilgrim: lowest (5)

Michael Price: NA

Douglas Ramos: average (3)

Brian Rogers: above average (2)

Eileen Rominger: average (3)

Robert Sanborn: above average (2)

Peter Schliemann: above average (2)

Ralph Seger: lowest (5)

Sandra Shrewsbury: below average (4)

Richard Strong: above average (2)

Heiko Thieme: average (3)

Peter Van Dyke: above average (2)

Donald Yacktman: average (3)

Responses: 27

Average: 2.88 (slightly above average)

Contrarians: Isabelle, Pilgrim, Seger (5), Kaufman (1)

Median growth, 3.2, versus median value, 2.92, versus median blend, 2.5

When you don't understand its movements

Panelist comments:

Bonnel (average): "If I don't understand a stock's movements I'm often tempted not to sell." If the price is soaring: "I figure that a short squeeze might occur soon." [In a short squeeze, investors who have sold stock short—bet that its price would go down—may be "squeezed" by investors who keep buying the stock, driving the price up and forcing short-sellers to buy at lofty levels. If you sell during a squeeze, you will be selling unnaturally high.]

Pilgrim (lowest): "That happens all the time, and the reason is that the securities market is full of transient influences that you're never going to be able to figure out. The market is frequently random in its behavior. During a `short squeeze,' we might sell a little, just to be opportunistic on a price basis."

Yacktman (lowest): "Stocks can go off into fairyland because people may be buying it just on the basis of its going up. They're stock-chasers. Often, it's not helpful to look at stock market fluctuations."

Unexpected responses. Perhaps growth players are dealing with thinner, more unpredictable stocks, which is why they don't try to understand their ups and downs.

Art Bonnel: average (3)
Rudy Carryl: lowest (5)
Robert Christensen: below average (4)
James Craig: lowest (5)
Maureen Cullinane: average (3)
Hugh Denison: below average (4)
Richard Fentin: lowest (5)
Mario Gabelli: average (3)
Peter Hagerman: below average (4)
Richard Huson: above average (2)
Warren Isabelle: highest (1)

Arnold Kaufman: above average (2)

Warren Lammert: average (3)

William Lippman/Bruce Baughman: NA

Thomas Marsico: above average (2)

Terry Milberger: above average (2)

Gary Pilgrim: lowest (5)

Douglas Ramos: highest (1)

Brian Rogers: below average (4)

Eileen Rominger: lowest (5)

Robert Sanborn: highest (1)

Peter Schliemann: average (3)

Ralph Seger: average (3)

Sandra Shrewsbury: average (3)

Richard Strong: average (3)

Heiko Thieme: below average (4)

Peter Van Dyke: lowest (5)

Donald Yacktman: lowest (5)

Responses: 27

Average: 3.33 (less than average)

Contrarians: Ramos, Isabelle (1); Carryl, Craig, Fentin, Pilgrim, Rominger, Van Dyke, Yacktman (5)

Median growth, 3.72, versus median value, 3.0

When the price falls significantly

Panelist comments:

Bonnel (highest): "I might sell. It would depend on the state of the industry the company was in and the overall condition of the market. If the fundamentals are strong, I prefer to hang onto the stock, trusting that it will bounce back."

Sanborn (lowest): "The price falling a lot isn't important as long as the underlying capital value remains roughly constant."

Shrewsbury (below average): "If I believe the long-term funda-mentals are still there, it's a tremendous opportunity to buy. The stocks are on sale. But if I felt that the price had slumped because of fundamental problems with the company, I would sell. One must play it on a case-by-case scenario. Every case is a little bit different."

Pilgrim (lowest): "A price drop by itself is not an excuse for selling. If the fundamentals remain good, we would hold on to the stock, although a large price fall might indicate that the fundamentals were no longer so strong."

Value players seem to be more accepting of bad news. Perhaps, as mentioned, they know their stocks better.

Art Bonnel: highest (1)

Rudy Carryl: above average (2)

Robert Christensen: below average (4)

James Craig: average (3)

Maureen Cullinane: average (3)

Hugh Denison: average (3)

Richard Fentin: below average (4)

Mario Gabelli: below average (4)

Peter Hagerman: above average (2)

Richard Huson: above average (2)

Warren Isabelle: lowest (5)

Arnold Kaufman: lowest (5)

Warren Lammert: above average (2)

William Lippman/Bruce Baughman: lowest (5)

Thomas Marsico: average (3)

Terry Milberger: average (3)

Gary Pilgrim: lowest (5)

Douglas Ramos: average (3)

Brian Rogers: below average (4)

Eileen Rominger: lowest (5)

Robert Sanborn: lowest (5)

Peter Schliemann: average (3)

Ralph Seger: above average (2)

Sandra Shrewsbury: below average (4)

Richard Strong: below average (4)

Heiko Thieme: lowest (5)

Peter Van Dyke: average (3)

Donald Yacktman: lowest (5)

Responses: 28

Average: 3.39 (less than average)

Contrarians: Thieme, Rominger, Pilgrim, Kaufman, Isabelle , Sanborn (5); Bonnel (1)

Median growth, 1.8, versus median value, 3.58

Chapter 14

Worst Mistakes

A mateurs buy at a stock's high and sell at its low. The pros make more subtle mistakes. They buy a stock too late—after it has rapidly run up. Or they sell it too soon—and miss further appreciation. Or they sell it too late—when the stock has already begun plummeting, probably because it was high-priced or because bad news was announced or imminent.

Growth investors and value investors evidently make markedly different mistakes. And by their mistakes you shall know them: This seems to be an important differentiation between the two types of investors.

In general, growth investors seem to hold on too long. The music begins to fade, but the ride has been so agreeable that they resist getting off the merry-go-round.

Value investors buy too soon (the stock's price proceeds to retreat some more) and sell too soon (the stock's price continues climbing). Being conservative investors, value investors prefer to take their birds in the hand.

Only two investors (Bonnel and Strong) confessed themselves guilty of buying too late—and both are growth investors. Value investors wouldn't make that mistake, apparently because stocks that go down tend to remain down for quite some time. Value investors have plenty of time to buy.

Perhaps the two self-designated blend managers whose biggest mistake is buying too soon, Hagerman and Yacktman, are really value investors. (Yacktman has a reputation for being a value investor.) And the two panelists whose biggest mistake is selling too late (Milberger and Lammert) may be basically growth investors. (A pure blend manager would have reported that his or her worst mistakes were buying too soon *and* selling too late.)

Most Common Mistakes

	All panelists	Growth	Value	Blend
Buying too soon	10		8	2
Buying too late	2	2		
Selling too soon	10	2	8	
Selling too late	11	8	1	2

What is your worst typical mistake?

Panelist comments:

Shrewsbury (growth): "I'm angry when I sell too late, not just because the price is down but because changing fundamental conditions mean that the price is unlikely to bounce back up. It's easy, when you know a company, to overlook things that are really changing. If you are overfamiliar with a stock, you may believe that the fundamentals will always stay strong. You might not realize that, `Gee! Things are really different and I should move out!' It's because of investors' attachments to certain stocks that technical analysis can be very useful. It can predict changes and provide for early-warning shifts in the broader market. There are times when the charts give you a clue that something really is going on here."

Pilgrim (growth): "Anytime you're becoming apprehensive about how a company is going, usually the smoke on the horizon is something you have to make a judgment about. One can wait too long to sell, and then you can make untimely sales. You could have done better if you'd been quicker with your finger on the trigger."

Seger (growth): "Assuming past growth will continue."

Art Bonnel: Buying too late, selling too late

Rudy Carryl: Selling too late

Robert Christensen: Selling too late

James Craig: Selling too soon

Maureen Cullinane: Selling too late

Hugh Denison: Selling too soon

Richard Fentin: "Selling too soon, not recognizing secular shift in company fundamentals"

Mario Gabelli: Buying too soon

Peter Hagerman: Buying too soon

Richard Huson: Selling too soon, buying too quickly

Warren Isabelle: Buying too soon

Arnold Kaufman: NA

Warren Lammert: Selling too late

William Lippman/Bruce Baughman: NA

Thomas Marsico: Buying companies developing a new product.

Terry Milberger: Selling too late

Gary Pilgrim: Selling too late

Michael Price: Selling too soon, buying too soon

Douglas Ramos: Buying too soon

Brian Rogers: Selling too soon, buying too soon

Eileen Rominger: Selling too soon

Robert Sanborn: Selling too soon, buying too soon

Peter Schliemann: Selling too soon, buying too soon

Ralph Seger: Selling too late

Sandra Shrewsbury: Selling too late

Richard Strong: Selling too soon, buying too late

Heiko Thieme: Selling too late

Peter Van Dyke: Selling too late

Donald Yacktman: Buying too soon

Totals: Selling too late (11), selling too soon (10), buying too soon (10), buying late (2)

Growth investors: selling too late (8), selling too soon (1), buying late (1)

Value investors: selling soon (7), buying soon (7), selling late (1)

Chapter 15

The Case for Modest Market Timing

Market timing—trying to avoid bear markets and enjoy bull markets—has a bad reputation, like astrology, or Scientology, or homeopathic medicine.

Extreme market timing probably deserves its poor reputation. Continual attempts to avoid mini-bear markets do seem fruitless. Besides, there are two vital decisons to be made: When to get out and when to get back in. And commissions can be devastating—unless you're investing in no-load mutual funds that allow you to move in and out at will, without charge.

Yet, while everyone seems to badmouth market timing, almost everyone seems to practice it—to a certain extent. Two of our leading newsletters, *The Value Line Investment Survey* and Standard & Poor's *The Outlook*, on the very first page of every issue, advise readers how much of their portfolios should be in stocks. *Money* magazine, while normally pushing a strict buy-and-hold policy in its pages, also runs articles recommending that people buy or sell stocks because of market conditions.

But it does not seem imprudent to practice occasional, limited market timing when the evidence is unusually clear that stocks are overvalued or undervalued. Modest market timing means raising one's usual level of cash when prices seem high, or moving over to more conservative stocks—or to short-term, high-rated bonds or to cash equivalents. Or, if one thinks stock prices are low, to use your cash and move into more volatile stocks. (Aggressive market timers would frequently buy puts, or sell short, when they think the market is overpriced, and buy calls or use leverage when they think the market is underpriced.)

Modest market timers would be guided by rather overt signals with regard to stocks: Price/earnings ratios, dividend yields, and price-book ratios. Aggressive market timers would be guided by more distant drummers: for example, subtle signs that the economy is about to slow down.

After the crash of 1987, a well known mutual fund manager—whose fund I owned shares of—told me that he had been convinced that the stock market had been frighteningly overvalued. Yet he had remained fully invested. That was what his fund family and what his shareholders expected of him, he told me. "But I told members of my church committee," he went on, "to get out of stocks." (After pondering this, I decided that I should have dropped out of his fund and joined his church.)

On another ocassion, I asked a portfolio manager whether he was a market timer or not. He laughed deprecatingly and said no, not at all. What a silly notion. I next asked how he was positioned. "I'm 60% in cash," he said, becoming serious and proceeding to explain why he thought the stock market was overvalued.

These days, almost everyone still sneers at market timing; yet the public continues to invest billions of dollars in market timing funds like Fidelity Asset Manager.

Our panelists generally described themselves as modest market timers: on a scale of 1 (none) to 5 (aggressive), they typically placed themselves just below 2.

Growth investors were more likely to look favorably upon market timing than value investors. This might have been expected in view of the fact that growth investors are quicker on the trigger in general. After all, one of the benefits of being a value investor is that such stocks are already so deep in the well that they don't have much farther to fall. And perhaps value investors markets time passively: When they cannot find enough undervalued stocks, they let cash build up.

For a fuller discussion of market timing, see Chapter 24 in my book, *The Ultimate Mutual Fund Guide*.

What kind of market timer are you—none (1) to aggressive (5)?

Panelist comments:

Bonnel (almost none): "I've been known to invest more conservatively sometimes, or to build up cash. But it would depend on whether I was managing my own money or other people's. If the money was my own and I was unhappy with the state of the market, I would try to build up cash. But when running a mutual fund, I have found that my clients tend to get agitated when I don't invest their money in stocks.

"The one time that I built up cash in a mutual fund was in 1992, when the market was depressed. But I found that you get no credit for being right, and clients did not really understand why I had done this. I also found it difficult to re-enter the market at the right time. We re-entered a tad late, after about six months of building up cash."

Art Bonnel: almost none (2)

Rudy Carryl: none (1)

Robert Christensen: medium (3)

James Craig: almost none (2)

Maureen Cullinane: almost none (2)

Hugh Denison: none (1)

Richard Fentin: none (1)

Mario Gabelli: none (1)

Peter Hagerman: medium (3)

Richard Huson: medium (3)

Warren Isabelle: none (1)

Arnold Kaufman: NA

Warren Lammert: almost none (2)

William Lippman/Bruce Baughman: none (1)

Thomas Marsico: almost none (2)

Terry Milberger: almost none (2)

Gary Pilgrim: none (1)

Michael Price: none (1)

Douglas Ramos: almost none (2)

Brian Rogers: almost none (2)

Eileen Rominger: almost none (2)

Robert Sanborn: none (1)

Peter Schliemann: none (1)

Ralph Seger: medium (3)

Sandra Shrewsbury: almost none (2)

Richard Strong: somewhat aggressive (4)

Heiko Thieme: somewhat aggressive (4)

Peter Van Dyke: almost none (2)

Donald Yacktman: none (1)

Respondents: 28

Average: 1.89

Contrarians: Strong (4), Thieme (4)

Median growth, 2.1, versus median value, 1.71

Chapter 16

The 25 Best Stocks to Buy and Hold

B elow, in alphabetical order, are the stocks that at least two of our 24 stock-market authorities recommended for buy-and-hold investors. The number of nominations the stocks received is in parentheses. The stocks recommended by the most panelists: General Electric (6), followed by Motorola (5).

AT&T (2), Bristol-Myers Squibb (2), Chevron (2), Citicorp (3), Coca-Cola (3), Dun & Bradstreet (2), Emerson Electric (3), Fannie Mae (3), Freddie Mac (2), General Electric (6), General Mills (2), General Motors (2), IBM (2), Intel (2), Merck (3), McDonald's (3), MCI Communications (3), Minnesota Mining (3), Motorola (5), (J.P.) Morgan (3), Pepsico (2), Pfizer (2), Philip Morris (3), UST (2), Wal-Mart (2).

If you want to create a portfolio of these stocks, be warned that some are in the same industry. Here is a breakdown of the industries:

Automobiles—General Motors
Banking—Citicorp, (J.P.) Morgan
Department stores—Wal-Mart
Diversified—Minnesota Mining
Food—Coca-Cola, General Mills, McDonald's, PepsiCo
Information services—Dun & Bradstreet
Mortgage lenders—Federal National Mortgage Association (Fannie Mae), Federal Home Loan Mortgage (Freddie Mac)
Oil—Chevron
Pharmaceuticals—Bristol-Myers Squibb, Merck & Co., Pfizer,
Technology—Emerson Electric, General Electric, IBM, Intel, Motorola

Telecommunications—AT&T, MCI
Tobacco—Philip Morris, UST

The information about the companies that follows was provided by
Standard & Poor's Corporation (25 Broadway, New York, New York
10004), and is copyrighted. Comments from our panelists on particular
stocks are included.

AT&T Corp.
Office: 32 Avenue of the Americas, New York, NY, 10013-2412
Telephone: 212-387-5400.
New York Stock Exchange
Symbol T
Industry: telecommunications
Member of Standard & Poor's 500
S&P Ranking: A+
Beta: 0.84
Reinvestment plan available
Dividends paid since 1881
Summary: AT&T is the largest U.S. long-distance telephone company.
It also manufactures telecommunications equipment and computers,
and provides financial services. In August 1993, the company an-
nounced a definitive agreement to acquire McCaw Cellular Com-
munications.

Bristol-Myers Squibb
"A proven company. Its current price doesn't reflect its prospects.
It will continue to grow."—Christensen
"This company has a quasi-monopoly over certain anticancer
drugs, especially with Capoten. In general, the drug industry has
patent protection, so the companies don't need as high a percentage
of the market share in order to be attractive."—Yacktman
Office: 345 Park Avenue, New York, NY, 10022
Telephone: 212-546-4000
New York Stock Exchange
Symbol: BMY
Industry: pharmaceuticals
Member of Standard & Poor's 500
S&P Ranking: A+
Beta: 0.98

Reinvestment plan available
Dividends paid since 1933
Summary: The company is one of the world's largest pharmaceutical concerns, with important drugs in cardiovascular, antiinfective, anticancer, and other areas. It also has interests in infant nutritions, nonprescription medications, medical devices, and toiletries.

Chevron Corp.
Office: 225 Bush Stret, San Francisco, CA, 94104-4289
Telephone: 415-894-7700
New York Stock Exchange
Symbol: CHV
Industry: petroleum
Member of Standard & Poor's 500
S&P Ranking: B
Beta: 0.56
Reinvestment plan available
Dividends paid since 1912
Summary: Chevron (formerly Standard Oil of California) is a worldwide petroleum company with important interests in chemicals and minerals. It is a leading U.S. producer of crude oil and natural gas, and a marketer of refined products. It is active in foreign exploration and production, and overseas refining and marketing. The company is restructuring its asset base to shift its exploration and production emphasis to foreign areas and to reshape U.S. refining and marketing. Profits in 1995 should rebound from weak 1994 levels, reflecting improvement in worldwide refined-product fundamentals, greater U.S. natural gas sales, and a stronger cost structure.

Citicorp
Office: 399 Park Avenue, New York, NY, 10043
Telephone: 212-559-1000
New York Stock Exchange
Symbol: CCI
Industry: banking
Member of Standard & Poor's 500
S&P Ranking: B-
Beta: 1.06
Dividends paid since 1994 (paid since 1813, suspended in 1991)

Summary: This company, the parent of Citbank, the largest bank in New York City and in the United States, has a substantial worldwide corporate and retail banking presence, as well as growing investment banking services. Following a large loss in 1991, earnings rebounded to record levels in 1993 and continued to rise in the first nine months of 1994, despite sharply lower trading revenues. With a lower cost structure and improved asset quality, further earnings growth is expected at least through 1995.

Coca-Cola
Office: 1 Coca-Cola Plaza, N.W., Atlanta, GA, 30313
Telephone: 404-676-2121
New York Stock Exchange
Symbol: KO
Industry: beverages
Member of Standard & Poor's 500
S&P Ranking: A+
Beta: 1.12
Reinvestment plan available
Dividends paid since 1893
Summary: Coca-Cola is the world's largest soft-drink company and has a sizable fruit-juice business. Its bottling interests include 44 percent ownership of New York Stock Exchange-listed Coca-Cola Enterprises. About 79 percent of 1993 operating profits came from international operations. Earnings are expected to continue in a strong uptrend through 1995, led by further, aggressive worldwide expansion.

Warren E. Buffett, one of the most admired investors of our day, is chairman of Berkshire Hathaway, which owns 7.3 percent of Coca-Cola stock.

Dun & Bradstreet
Office: 200 Nyala Farms, Wesport, CT. 06880
Telephone: 203-222-4200
New York Stock Exchange
Symbol: DNB
Industry: information services
Member of Standard & Poor's 500
S&P Ranking: A

Beta: 0.74

Dividends paid since 1934

Summary: The company is best known for its risk management and business-marketing information services, which include D&B Business Credit Services, Moody's, and Interactive Data. Services also include marketing information (Nielson and IMS International), telephone directory information, and computer software. DNB expects restructuring steps taken in 1992 and 1993 to enable it to realize annual pre-tax cost savings of $100 million within a few years, which will be largely used for measures to accelerate revenue growth.

Emerson Electric

"Outstanding long-term record, which will continue. Although Emerson has appreciated so that its price/earnings ratio is in the middle, it's about equal to the S&P 500."—Christensen

Office: 8000 W. Florissant Avenue, St. Louis, MO, 63136

Telephone: 314-553-2000

New York Stock Exchange

Symbol: EMR

Industry: technology

Member of Standard & Poor's 500

S&P Ranking: A+

Beta: 1.23

Reinvestment plan available

Dividends paid since 1947

Summary: This long-established manufacturer of electrical and electronic products has compiled an outstanding record of consistent earnings and dividend growth. EMR has an active program of acquisitions and divestitures. Earnings rose again in fiscal 1993, aided by acquisitions, new products, and well-controlled costs. A substantial increase in fiscal 1994 should reflect higher-capital spending, stronger economic growth, and a nonrecurring gain. In the absence of this gain, an earnings decline is likely in fiscal 1995, despite continued operating improvements.

Federal National Mortgage Association

Office: 3900 Wisconsin Ave., N.W., Washington, D.C., 20016

Telephone: 202-752-7000

New York Stock Exchange

Symbol: FNM
Industry: mortgage lender
Member of Standard & Poor's 500
S&P Ranking: A-
Beta: 1.64
Reinvestment plan available
Dividends paid since 1956
Summary: Fannie Mae, a U.S. government-sponsored, publicly held company, is the largest mortgage lender in the United States. It uses mostly borrowed funds to buy a variety of mortgages, thereby creating a secondary market for mortgage lenders. The company has only one major competitor and a number of much smaller competitors in its major markets. Double-digit earnings and dividend growth are expected to continue for the foreseeable future.

Federal Home Loan Mortgage
Office: 8200 Jones Branch Drive, McLean, VA, 22102
Telephone: 703-903-2000
New York Stock Exchange
Symbol: FRE
Industry: mortgages
Member of Standard & Poor's 500
S&P Ranking: NA
Beta: NA
Dividends paid since 1989
Summary: Freddie Mac, a corporate instrumentality of the U.S. Government, buys mortgages from lenders, pools and packages the mortgages into securities, and sells those securities to investors. The company typically posts a quarterly return on equity of over 20% A long uptrend in earnings is expected to continue for the foreseeable future, aided by growth in the mortgage portfolio FRE owns and increased securitization of mortgage originations.

General Electric
Office: 3135 Easton Turnpike, Fairfield, CT, 06431
Telephone: 203-373-2211
New York Stock Exchange
Symbol: GE

Industry: services, technology, manufacturing
Member of Standard & Poor's 500
S&P Ranking: A+
Beta: 1.2
Reinvestment plan available
Dividends paid since 1889
Summary: General Electric's major businesses include aircraft engines, medical systems, power systems, broadcasting, appliances, lighting, and financial services. Aerospace operations were sold to Martin Marietta early in 1993. Despite strong operating improvement, earnings from continuing operations rose only modestly in 1993, due to restructuring changes. A $210 million charge for irregular trading activities at its Kidder Peabody subsidiary will restrain the expected gain in earnings, despite major operating improvements. Sharply higher earnings are likely in 1995.

General Mills
Office: Number One General Mills Blvd., Minneapolis, MN, 55426
Telephone: 612-540-2311
New York Stock Exchange
Symbol: GIS
Industry: foods
Member of Standard & Poor's 500
S&P Ranking: A
Beta: 0.99
Reinvestment plan available
Dividends paid since 1898
Summary: The leading producer of branded consumer foods also owns the Red Lobster and Olive Garden restaurant chains. Earnings for 1993-94 were penalized by a $0.55-a-share fourth-quarter decline related to disposing of improperly treated oat products. A related decline in shipments hurt 1994-95 first-quarter results. With cereal operations reportedly restored to normal, profit growth should resume.

Products include breakfast cereals (Cheerios, Wheaties, Lucky Charms, Total), baking mixes (Betty Crocker, Potato Buds), snacks (Pop Secret, Bugles, Squeezit), Gorton's seafood entrees, Yoplait, and Columbo yogurt.

General Motors
Office: 3044 West Grand Blvd., Detroit, MI, 48202
Telephone: 313-556-5000
New York Stock Exchange
Symbol: GM
Industry: automobiles
Member of Standard & Poor's 500
S&P Ranking: B-
Beta: 0.77
Reinvestment plan available
Dividends paid since 1915
Summary: The world's largest manufacturer of cars and trucks (Chevrolet, Buick, Cadillac, Oldsmobile, Pontiac, GEO, Saturn), GM continues its efforts to reduce costs and excess capacity, even as it benefits from a strong domestic vehicle market. Considerable progress was made in 1993, but challenges include an expensive labor contract and market-share erosion in North America as GM continues to reduce its fleet vehicle sales. But sharply improved earnings are likely for 1994 due to the overall strengthening of North American vehicle markets and stable profits in overseas markets. Further improvement is expected in 1995.

International Business Machines
Office: Old Orchard Road, Armonk, New York, NY, 10504
Telephone: 914-765-1900
New York Stock Exchange
Symbol: IBM
Industry: technology
Member of Standard & Poor's 500
S&P Ranking: B-
Beta: 0.50
Reinvestment plan available
Dividends paid since 1916
Summary: IBM is the world's dominant manufacturer of mainframe computers and a major supplier of minicomputers, computer peripheral equipment, personal computers, networking products, and system software. IBM has engineered a successful earnings turnaround in recent quarters, fueled by substantial expense

reductions and an improving sales trend. Continued favorable earnings comparisons are expected through at least 1995.

Intel
Office: 2200 Mission College Blvd., Santa Clara, CA, 95052-8119
Telephone: 408-765-8080
NASDAQ
Symbol: INTC
Industry: semiconductors
Member of Standard & Poor's 500
S&P Ranking: B
Beta: 1.5
Dividends paid since 1992
Summary: The world's leading semiconductor manufacturer, this company produces microcomputer components, modules, and systems. Its business is closely tied to the computer industry, especially the personal computer segment. Following three years of strong growth, earnings more than doubled in 1993. Slower growth in the personal computer industry and increasing competition in the microprocessor market should result in more moderate earnings increases in 1994 and 1995. A common share-repurchase program was recently expanded.

MCI Communications
Office: 1801 Pennsylvania Ave., NW, Washington, D.C., 20006
Telephone: 202-872-2028
NASDAQ
Symbol: MCIC
Industry: telecommunications
S&P Ranking: B
Beta: 1.25
Summary: MCI is the second largest U.S. long-distance telephone carrier. As part of its long-term strategic plan to profitably grow its core business, expand globally, and enter new markets, the company has announced plans to upgrade its network, enter the local telephone market, and enter the Canadian and Mexican markets through strategic alliances. MCI has also formed a strategic alliance with British Telecommunications to provide advanced global

communications; BT will also purchase a 20 percent interest in the company for $4.3 billion.

McDonald's Corp.

"It's been a tremendous growth story for years and years. And they have been expanding into nontraditional areas for food outlets: airports and so forth. So there is a lot of room for them to continue growing at a fast rate. There is tremendous potential both nationally and internationally."—Shrewsbury

Office: McDonald's Plaza, Oak Brook, IL, 60521
Telephone: 708-575-3000
New York Stock Exchange
Symbol: MCD
Industry: Fast-food restaurants
Member of Standard & Poor's 500
S&P Ranking: A+
Beta: 1.08
Reinvestment plan available
Dividends paid since 1976

Summary: Aggressive expansion and creative merchandising over the years have enabled McDonald's to maintain its position as the dominant force in the fast-food industry. International operations are expected to fuel much of MCD's sales and operating profit growth. However, a "value" strategy appears to be helping its sales in the United States, where about 66 percent of MCD's systemwide units are located. A two-for-one stock split was effected in June 1994.

Merck & Co.

"It fits the pattern of what we're looking for. A high return on assets, for example." — Yacktman

Office: One Merck Drive, P.O. Box 100, Whitehouse Station, NJ, 08889
Telephone: 908-423-1000
New York Stock Exchange
Symbol: MRK
Industry: pharmaceuticals
Member of Standard & Poor's 500
S&P Ranking: A+
Beta: 1.13
Reinvestment plan available
Dividends paid since 1935

Summary: Merck is the world's largest ethical drug manufacturer, producing a wide range of human and animal pharmaceuticals. In November 1993, the company acquired Medco Containment Services, the leading mail-order drug marketer in the United States, for about $6.6 billion in cash and stock. Although initially dilutive, the acquisition has strengthened the company's position in the expanding managed-care market and should enhance earnings growth in the years ahead.

Minnesota Mining

"Well diversified, both domestically and internationally. Spead out over healthcare products, sandpaper, Post-It notes, chemicals, and other such products that generally sell well during and after an economic upturn."—Shrewsbury

"Very good earnings and dividend growth, and the stock hasn't done well over the past three years."—Rogers

Office: 3M Center, St. Paul, MN, 55144
Telephone: 612-733-1110
New York Stock Exchange
Symbol: MMM
Industry: Scotch tapes, coated abrasives
Member of Standard & Poor's 500
S&P Ranking: A+
Beta: 0.72
Reinvestment plan available
Dividends paid since 1916
Summary: MMM is a highly diversified manufacturer of industrial, commercial, healthcare, and consumer products that share similar technological, manufacturing, and marketing resources. Earnings gains for 1993 were restricted by unfavorable currency translation, recession in Europe and Japan, and pricing pressures. However, improving worldwide economic conditions should lead to more favorable sales and earnings comparisons in the second half of 1994 and through 1995.

(J.P.) Morgan & Co.

"It has a world franchise and it's very inexpensive."—Rogers
Office: 60 Wall Street, New York, NY, 10260-0060
Telephone: 212-483-2323
New York Stock Exchange

Symbol: JPM
Industry: banking
Member of Standard & Poor's 500
S&P Ranking: B+
Beta: 1.25
Reinvestment plan available
Dividends paid since 1892
Summary: This bank-holding company, the third largest in the United States, owns Morgan Guaranty Trust. JPM emphasizes corporate finance, asset management, operational services, and trading, investing, and managing risk in global markets. International operations in more than 40 countries accounted for 69 percent of 1993 net income. Sharply higher noninterest income, led by exceptional trading revenues and improved asset quality, resulted in record earnings in 1993. With a decline in trading revenues likely in a volatile capital-markets environment, lower earnings were expected for 1994.

Motorola, Inc.

"A very well-diversified company in the technology and communications area. It's a well established company to participate in those areas."—Shrewsbury
Office: 1303 E. Algonquin Rd., Schaumburg, IL, 60196
Telephone: 708-576-5000
New York Stock Exchange
Symbol: MOT
Industry: technology
Member of Standard & Poor's 500
S&P Ranking: A
Beta: 1.19
Dividends paid since 1942
Summary: Motorola is the leading supplier of semiconductors and two-way radios, paging equipment, and cellular mobile telephone systems. Other products include information systems, government electronics and automobile and industrial electronics. Following substantially higher earnings in 1992, much greater profits were reported in 1993, reflecting broad-based strength. Demand remains strong, with economic growth accelerating and new products being introduced aggressively.

PepsiCo, Inc.
Office: 700 Anderson Hill Rd., Purchase, NY, 10577
Telephone: 914-253-2000
New York Stock Exchange
Symbol: PEP
Industry: beverages
Member of Standard & Poor's 500
S&P Ranking: A+
Beta: 1.13
Reinvestment plan available
Dividends paid since 1952
Summary: PepsiCo. is a major worldwide producer of beverage products and snack foods, and a leading operator and franchisor of restaurants with its Pizza Hut, Taco Bell, and KFC chains. Foreign operations accounted for 27 percent of sales and 18 percent of profits in 1993. Earnings are expected to continue their long upward climb through 1995, led by further snack foods volume gains.

Pfizer Inc.
Office: 235 East 42nd St., New York, NY, 10017
Telephone: 212-573-2323
New York Stock Exchange
Symbol: PFE
Industry: pharmaceuticals
Member of Standard & Poor's 500
S&P Ranking: A+
Beta: 1.46
Reinvestment plan available
Dividends paid since 1901
Summary: This leading ethical pharmaceutical producer also has important positions in hospital products, animal health items, non-prescription medications and food ingredients. Despite increased industrywide constraints on drug pricing and intensified competition in global pharmaceutical markets, earnings are expected to expand in the years ahead, aided by an impressive array of new drugs.

Philip Morris
"It meets all of our criteria. The price has been cheap, the value

of the company has been growing, and management is buying up stock. And the management is decent."—Sanborn

"It has almost 50 percent of the domestic cigarette business, and it's the engine that allows other parts of the company to grow, like General Foods."—Yacktman
Office: 120 Park Ave., New York, NY, 10017
Telephone: 212-880-5000
New York Stock Exchange
Symbol: MO
Industry: cigarettes, food, beer
Member of Standard & Poor's 500
S&P Ranking: A+
Beta: 1.18
Reinvestment plan available
Dividends paid since 1928
Summary: Philip Morris is the largest cigarette company in the United States, the largest U.S. food processor (Kraft General Foods), and the second largest brewer (Miller Brewing). Earnings per share are expected to continue the rebound from 1993's depressed levels, led by improved U.S. cigarette selling prices and product mix, recent restructuring initiatives, and a resumption in stock repurchases. In August 1994, MO hiked the quarterly dividend 20 percent and authorized a new three-year share repurchase program worth $6.0 billion.

UST Inc.

"They have an 80 percent share of the market and a low p/e. Controlling the market, either through market share or patents in specific areas, is important."—Yacktman
Office: 100 West Putnam Ave., Greenwich, CT, 06830
Telephone: 203-661-1100
New York Stock Exchange
Symbol: UST
Industry: tobacco
Member of Standard & Poor's 500
S&P Ranking: A+
Beta: 1.10
Reinvestment plan available
Dividends paid since 1912

Summary: UST is a leading producer of moist smokeless tobacco products under such leading brand names as Copenhagen and Skoal. To a much lesser extent, the company also produces and sells wine and other products. Assuming the absence of a significantly higher federal excise tax on tobacco and wine products, UST's share earnings through 1995 are expected to grow at a strong pace, led by further sales volume growth and higher selling prices for moist smokeless tobacco products and continued aggressive stock repurchases.

Wal-Mart Stores
Office: 702 Southwest 8th St., Bentonville, AZ, 72716
Telephone: 501-273-4000
New York Stock Exchange
Symbol: WMT
Industry: department stores
Member of Standard & Poor's 500
S&P Ranking: A+
Beta: 1.13
Dividends paid since 1973
Summary: Wal-Mart is the largest retailer in the United States, operating a chain of discount department stores primarily spanning the Sunbelt and the Midwest, with more recent expansion on the East and West Coasts and in Mexico and Canada. Although slow growth in consumer spending and a larger store base should temper sales gains, larger store formats, aggressive pricing, and new store openings should continue to facilitate market-share gains.

Chapter 17

The Single Best Stock to Buy

S eventeen of the panelists named a single best stock — one of them only on the condition of anonymity. (That panelist believes that recommending a single stock is too risky.)

Only General Electric and Philip Morris were mentioned by two different panelists.

Here are the panelists' favorite stocks:

AT&T—Douglas Ramos
American Recreation Centers—Peter Schliemann
American Management Systems—Peter Van Dyke
General Electric—Richard Fentin
General Electric—Peter Hagerman
General Motors—Richard Strong
IBM—Richard Huson
Merrill Lynch—Thomas Marsico
MGIC—Hugh Denison
Motorola—Sandra Shrewsbury
Philip Morris—Robert Sanborn
Philip Morris—Heiko Thieme
Plum Creek Timber—Robert Christensen
UST—anonymous
United Asset Management—Yacktman
United Healthcare—Rudy Carryl
WalMart—James Craig

One comment:
"There is nothing I would buy and hold. Times change, and so do companies."—Art Bonnel

Chapter 18

Best and Worst Industries

Telecommunications, not surprisingly, is one industry that most panelists were sure would thrive in the next few years. Technology and drugs were also favorites. Even tobacco received one nomination.

The industries most often named for decline were electrical utilities and major pharmaceuticals.

Here are tabulations of industries the panelists thought would thrive or decline, followed by the individual selections:

Industries that Should Thrive
Telecommunications/wireless communications/long distance/
   networking (14)
Technology (electronics, office equipment, semiconductors) (8)
Drugs (4)
Real Estate Investment Trusts (REITs) (3)
Capital goods (3)
Transaction processing/financial services (2)
Biotechnology (1)
Video (1)
Natural gas (1)
Select retail (1)
Security (1)
Commodities: steel, aluminum, gold, oil (1)
Multimedia (1)
Pollution control (1)
Long-term care (1)
Entertainment (1)
Food (1)
Tobacco (1)
Media (1)
Household products (1)

Which industries do you think will grow apace over the next several years?

Art Bonnell: Computers, drugs, networking, video
"The drug industry seems to have survived the attack Clinton launched against it. The healthcare issue seems to be waning, and the drug companies seem to be coming back. Moreover, as the population continues to age, the drug companies and their products are going to be increasingly in demand."

Rudy Carryl: Health care services, technology

Robert Christensen: Natural gas

James Craig: Transaction processing; select retail; long distance

Maureen Cullinane: Technology (electronics, office equipment), capital goods

Hugh Denison: Telecomunications, security, financial services

Richard Fentin: Commodities: steel, aluminum, gold, oil

Mario Gabelli: Telecommunications, multimedia, quality, low-cost manufacturers with international distribution.

Peter Hagerman: Wireless communications, semiconductors, pollution control

Richard Huson: "Many areas of technology, and REITs."

Warren Isabelle: Telecommunications, biotechnology

Arnold Kaufman: NA

Warren Lammert: Telecommunications

William Lippman/Bruce Baughman: NA

Thomas Marsico: Communications

Terry Milberger: Telecommunications, long-term care

Gary Pilgrim: NA

Douglas Ramos: Telecommunications, personal computer, computer networks

Brian Rogers: NA

Eileen Rominger: NA

Robert Sanborn: Communications; software; entertainment; medical

Peter Schliemann: NA

Ralph Seger: Communications/computer interaction. ("It is much better to find the best managed individual company rather than look at a growing industry.")

Sandra Shrewsbury: Technology

Richard Strong: "We believe there is a shift under way in the economy that will favor many cyclical, basic-industry, and capital-goods stocks during a good part of the 1990s, following a period of severe underinvestment in this sector during the 1980s. Other industries that look attractive include software, radio broadcasting, entertainment, and selected REITs."

Heiko Thieme: Pharmaceuticals, telecommunications, interactive technology

Peter Van Dyke: Communications, software, real estate

Donald Yacktman: Apparel/shoes, drugs, food, household products, media, tobacco

Industries that Should Decline
Drugs/major pharmaceuticals (7)
Electrical utilities (7)
Commodities (copper, steel, precious metals) 5
Food (3)
Retail (2)
Branded consumer products 2
Airlines (1)
Heavy industries (1)
Autos (1)
Computers (mainframe) 2
Autos (1)
Soft drinks (1)
Tobacco (domestic) (2)
Cable (1)
Coal (1)
Fancy footwear (1)
Medical supplies (1)

Which industries do you think will decline?

Art Bonnell: Major industries—steel, food, autos

"Currently it looks like the auto industry is running `full bore,' and the old theory is that if the basic industries are working overtime, without more capital investment, the indications are that one should sell."

Rudy Carryl: Drugs

Robert Christensen: Mining and metals

James Craig: Cable, electric utilities, medical supplies

Maureen Cullinane: Major pharmaceuticals

Hugh Denison: Retailers, branded consumer products
Richard Fentin: Food, drugs, consumer cyclicals
Mario Gabelli: NA
Peter Hagerman: Electric utilities, coal, fashion footwear (sneakers)
Richard Huson: Healthcare, soft drinks, tobacco
Warren Isabelle: Retail
Arnold Kaufman: NA
Warren Lammert: NA
William Lippman/Bruce Baughman: NA
Thomas Marsico: Electric utilities
Terry Milberger: Drug industry, food industry
Gary Pilgrim: NA
Douglas Ramos: Mainframe computers, minicomputers
Brian Rogers: NA
Eileen Rominger: NA
Robert Sanborn: Electrical utilities; basic banking; mutual funds
(perhaps)
Peter Schliemann: NA
Ralph Seger: Commodity-types—Steel, copper
Sandra Shrewsbury: Utilities; domestic tobacco; mainframe
computers
Richard Strong: "Many consumer nondurable stocks; selected
medical stocks; utilities."
Heiko Thieme: Precious metals
Peter Van Dyke: Aerospace, retailing
Donald Yacktman: Commodities, airlines, heavy industries, autos
"The common thread we've found is that good businesses tend to
have low capital intensity. All of the above, by contrast, have high
capital intensity because of their large asset bases. This makes it harder
for the industry to turn a profit.

"They can't compound money very rapidly. Stocks, in effect, are
variable-rate bonds, and the industries above do not have very high
returns on the investment.

"Take the airlines: If you add up all the earnings of all the airline
companies since Kitty Hawk, the industry has a loss—despite being a
continually growing industry in terms of units."

In predicting that these industries will decline, Yackman simply
meant that they grow at a slower pace than other industries.

Chapter 19

The Most Admired
Money Managers

A sked to name the money managers they admired most, the panelists tended to choose their colleagues, or the better-known names among investors (like Peter Lynch and Warren Buffett). And they tended to mention people who invest the same way they do.

The money manager named most often (eight nominations) was Buffett, who runs the Berkshire Hathaway Company. Second was Peter Lynch (four nominations), the former manager of Fidelity Magellan. William Ruane of the Sequoia Fund was third with three nominations. John Neff, the former manager of Vanguard/Windsor, was named twice.

Two panelists were named by other panelists. Craig was named by his Janus colleague, Warren Lammert; Yacktman by Sanborn ("His style is similar to ours—very disciplined, unemotional, and he sticks to his game plan.")

Several other managers also named their colleagues—Maureen Cullinane named a portfolio manager at Keystone, and Richard Huson named Jim Crabbe at the Crabbe Huson funds.

Famous managers of the past were generally ignored: Sir John Templeton, T. Rowe Price, Bernard Baruch. But Hugh Denison did mention Benjamin Graham, the father of value investing.

A few nominees are not well known.

Money Managers	*Recommended by Panelists*
John Neff, Jim Crabbe	Richard Huson
Ken Heebner	Douglas Ramos
Warren Buffett, John Neff	Peter S. Hagerman
Peter Lynch, Ralph Wanger	Peter C. Schliemann

Money Managers	Recommended by Panelists
William Ruane	Michael F. Price
Warren Buffett, George Soros	James P. Craig
James P. Craig	Warren B. Lammert
Peter Lynch	Art Bonnel
Warren Buffett, Benjamin Graham	Hugh Denison
Warren Buffett	William Lippman
Warren Buffett	Ralph L. Seger Jr.
Don Yacktman, Bill Durron (Skyline), Chuck Bath (Nationwide)	Robert Sanborn
Jim Capra	Thomas Marsico
Warren Buffett, William Ruane, Jim Gibson (Clipper Fund)	Donald Yacktman
Warren Buffett	Richard Strong
Peter Lynch, Warren Buffett	Arnold Kaufman
Roland Gillis (Keystone AG)	Maureen Cullinane
Peter Lynch	Rudy Carryl
Seth Klarman (a Boston manager and author), William Ruane, Shelby Davis (Selected American)	Brian C. Rogers

Chapter 20

Interviews with Panelists

Twenty-three of our panelists (with Lippman and Baughman counting as one) participated in interviews focusing on the issues addressed in this book. In alphabetical order, they are: Arthur J. Bonnel, Rudy Carryl, Robert A. Christensen, Maureen E. Cullinane, Hugh F. Denison, Richard Fentin, Mario Gabelli, Peter S. Hagerman, Richard S. Huson, Warren J. Isabelle, Warren B. Lammert, William Lippman/Bruce Baughman, Terry Milberger, Gary Pilgrim, Michael F. Price, Douglas Ramos, Brian C. Rogers, Eileen P. Rominger, Robert Sanborn, Peter C. Schliemann, Sandra Shrewsbury, Richard Strong, Donald T. Yacktman

Excerpts from these sessions follow.

Arthur J. Bonnel: Bonnel Growth Fund

Q. What is your strategy?

A. Anything is fair game—IBM, Chevron, Microsoft, Frederick's of Hollywood. And we look for companies that are earning more money this year than last year. That's a simple rule that can spare you a lot of pain and grief.

If a company passes that test, we use three other tests. We look at the ratio of current assets to current liabilities. We want a good balance sheet. We also look at long-term debt, which shouldn't be more than 25 percent of a stock's capitalization. We want companies that have money to grow, not just to pay down interest.

We also look at price/earnings ratios, return on equity, cash flow, and so forth.

And we want companies where the managers own the stock—5 percent to 20 percent—and where they've been adding to their positions. A lot may exercise options, but those options may not amount to a major part of their holdings.

We've been using this system for 20 years, and our return has been 18 percent to 20 percent a year, compounded.

Q. What's the benefit of being in Reno, Nevada, rather than the New York area?

A. We're not in the Wall Street rumor mill. We want to do our own research in-house and not listen to outside analysts. Besides, I run this business out of my home. So we don't spend our time at committee meetings, and there aren't constant interruptions.

Rudy Carryl: MainStay Capital Appreciation

Q. What is your strategy?

A. We look for companies with above-average growth and acceleration. They must be trading at a reasonable value compared with their earnings growth.

If a stock is growing at 25 percent a year and its price/earnings ratio is only 20, other things being equal, it's a good value. We want a growth rate higher than the price/earnings multiple—again, other things being equal.

We don't invest in companies with market caps below $100 million. We prefer companies that are more liquid.

Q. When do you sell?

A. When there's a change in the fundamentals. Perhaps the growth decelerates. Or there's a delay in a new product—which is common in health and technology. We'll put such a stock on our watch list.

We'll also put a stock on our watch list if its price/earnings ratio goes out of line with the growth rate and it seems to become too expensive.

And we take heed of what the market is telling us. If other investors aren't enthusiastic about a stock, and its relative strength isn't impressive, we'll revaluate the stock.

Q. Why has your fund been so successful?

A. We've stuck to our discipline, both on the buy side and the sell side. Also, we have a team approach, and each of our portfolio managers is a specialist in an industry.

Another reason for our success is that we stick to a bottom-up approach, looking only for growing companies.

Finally, we aren't restricted to buying only mid-cap or large-cap stocks. We can invest in any stocks above $100 million in market cap.

Robert A. Christensen: SteinRoe Total Return

Q. What is your strategy?

A. First, we look for a dividend income at least equal to the Standard & Poor's 500. That way, our average yield is a good bit higher than the S&P. Next, we look at capitalization [price times number of shares outstanding—a measure of company size]. The big-cap stocks are less volatile. Only 5 percent to 10 percent of our portfolio has a market cap under $1 billion.

Beyond that, we look for growth of income—whether or not the company will be increasing its dividends.

And beyond those three screens, we look for diversification. Normally, we have 50 stocks in our portfolio, and we keep them an average of three or four years.

Q. Do you own bonds?

A. We normally have 10 percent to 20 percent in bonds, to provide above-average yields and below-average volatility. Bonds are vulnerable to rising interest rates, but everything is vulnerable to rising rates.

Q. Do equity-income funds like yours have too broad a mandate?

A. Actually, it's the growth and income category that's all over the map. If the Standard & Poor's 500 is in the middle and everything to the left is less risky, then balanced funds and equity-income funds are on the left, growth-and-income funds are in the center, and capital-appreciation funds are on the right.

Maureen E. Cullinane: Keystone American Omega Fund A

Q. Would you describe your fund?

A. We have a great deal of flexibility. We can invest in all kinds of stocks—though we generally don't invest in very small companies. But we could go all the way up to Exxon if we wanted to. Generally, we're one-third in big caps, one-third in mid caps, and one-third in small caps over $100 million.

We emphasize earnings momentum. We want stocks growing faster than the S&P 500, particularly in technology, capital goods, and energy—from natural gas to oil and oil service.

Q. Why has your fund done so well?

A. We have a team of good analysts, and they've done a good job in selecting stocks. Each of them covers two or three industries, and they're always on the road looking at companies and making earnings estimates. Our analysts are also very realistic, and call them as they see them.

We concentrate on a limited number of companies and sectors. We're roughly in 50 stocks. And we put our maximum behind them.

Q. What percentage of your choices are successful?

A. It depends on the year. We like to have two-thirds of our choices be successful. But 60 percent is very good. One old portfolio manager has said that if as many as 90 percent of your choices are successful, you're not making enough choices. If only 40 percent or 50 percent of your choices are successful, you may be making too many choices—or not doing enough analytical work.

Q. When do you sell?

A. On earnings disappointments. And sometimes we'll reduce our exposure if a company reaches our target price. Or reassess the stock.

Hugh F. Denison: Heartland Value Fund

Q. What's the secret of your success?

A. Sheer brilliance. Actually, we operate in the small end of the small-cap market—our stocks have an average of less than $50 million in market capitalization. So a great many stocks that we own are totally unknown.

LSC Industries, for example, is a magazine-fulfillment company. It traded at $4–$5 seemingly forever. In early 1992, the stock suddenly went to $16, even though the company was doing neither better nor worse. What happened was that Wall Street picked up the idea and the stock went from horribly undervalued to richly overvalued. Our average cost in buying it was $4.50, and we sold it at $11, $12, and up to $16. It's down to $6 now. And we've been blessed with a fair amount of that activity in the last few years.

Q. When do you sell?

A. Our buy and our sell disciplines are similar. We have a rigid set of 10 parameters—price/earnings ratio, the rate of cash flow, book value, indebtedness, if the owners are buying or selling shares, and so forth. If a stock jumps up substantially, it tends to meet fewer of our criteria, so we may sell.

Q. Would you discourage individual investors from buying small-company stocks apart from mutual funds?

A. Yes, because few of them can have a diversified portfolio—we usually have 55 stocks—and because they don't have the time or the sophistication to analyze such stocks.

Richard Fentin: Fidelity Puritan

When, at the tender age of 31, Richard Fentin left Fidelity Growth (assets: $300 million) to take over the reins at the old Fidelity Puritan Fund (assets: $4 billion), he was worried. "I would have been inhuman if I hadn't been," he says now. Many shareholders were worried, too: Puritan's previous manager, Francis Cabour, had been well respected. And Fentin was so young!

Since then Fenton has amply proved himself: The fund has returned about 14.6 percent a year over the past 10 years.

Yet his success amid widespread worry has not left Fentin particularly smug. Asked when he first became sure that he could manage a fund as large as Puritan, he replied: "I've never become self-confident. In this business, you're proved wrong every day in so many ways. Mistakes are part of the job. What you try to do is not make the same mistakes."

He's made the same mistakes everyone else has. Falling in love with a stock, for example. He's bought a stock at $9 and watched it climb to $36 as the whole world began to recognize its true value. At that point "It's so pretty to have in your portfolio—even if you know it's now fairly priced or even overpriced." Then, suddenly, the horses turn into mice again, the coach into a pumpkin. "An expensive lesson," Fentin calls it.

Another mistake: Buying falling stars when they're down 50 percent. Then watching as they go down another 50 percent. "It's like trying to catch a falling sword," he says.

Still, mistakes come with the territory. "You have to make decisions quickly," he says. "If you wait until you have 100 percent perfect information, that would be built into the price of the stock."

Balanced funds like Puritan have been criticized as neither fish nor fowl, owning as they do stocks as well as bonds. Some observers go so far as to argue that investors should avoid balanced funds, buying individual stock funds and fixed-income funds instead.

But balanced funds have a built-in strength: They must shift around their holdings when they're out of whack. If they're supposed to be 60 percent in stocks and 40 percent in bonds, they must buy bonds when they constitute (say) only 25 percent of the portfolio, they must sell stocks when they rise to (say) 80 percent. This forces a balanced fund to veer in the direction of buying underpriced securities and selling overpriced securities.

Fentin agrees. While his fund may have only 50 percent in equities at certain times, and may go as high as 80 percent, it's rare for him to go to such extremes. And his need to balance his portfolio forces him to avoid high-priced securities. Several years ago, for example, his fund had 75 percent of its assets in U.S. stocks. In 1993, when he thought stocks were fairly valued, his U.S. stock portfolio was down to 35 percent.

"I never start the year with rigid guidelines," he goes on, thinking (for example) that he should be 65 percent in stocks and 35 percent in bonds. "I buy stocks stock-by-stock. If they're expensive, I sell out. If they're cheap, I'm happy to buy more."

Why has his fund done so well? One reason is that, as a value investor, he uses an unusually broad definition—and therefore can choose from a wider universe of stocks than many other value investors.

As he sees it, stocks can be cheap in three ways:

1. Statistically cheap. They sell at their net working capital, or for three times cash flow, or for half of their book value.

2. Cyclically cheap. Autos, steels, and other economically sensitive stocks are likely to be good buys when the economy is punk and their prices are way down.

3. Sometimes blue-chip companies come under a cloud, and temporarily become bargains compared to their usual valuations. Philip Morris is an example. Recently, Fentin bought it when its price came way down—and it's a stock he hadn't owned since after the 1987 crash. Healthcare stocks, he adds, "are also now in our universe." On the other hand, "companies like General Electric rarely get statistically cheap, but are generally good values after stock market declines."

He's also not averse to seeking undervalued stocks abroad, which allows him still more leeway. Recently, he was 35 percent in U.S. stocks and 15 percent in foreign equities. That was his lowest exposure to U.S. equities ever—and foreign stocks allowed him to do it.

In sum, because of his unusually wide universe, Fentin can find more and better underpriced stocks than many of his competitors.

Another advantage he cites: working for a gigantic organization like Fidelity, where 20 or more companies come to visit every day, and where the managers enjoy the renown and the clout that throws open doors to the top managements of other companies.

Fidelity, Fentin continues, also provides good training. "You can get lots of exposure to managing over the years," says Fentin, who joined Fidelity as a summer intern in 1979, "and there's no GroupThink, so everyone develops his own style. You get lots of responsibility early."

Since Fentin took over Puritan, the fund has grown from $4 billion to $8.5 billion. It hasn't changed his style. He still owns about 200 stocks. But the size of the companies may have become larger: From a minimum of $200 million in market capitalization to a minimum of $300 to $400 million now. [Market capitalization equals price times shares outstanding.]

What's it like, being forever in the shadow of that giant, Fidelity Magellan? "I root for him [manager Jeff Vinik] every day," Fentin replies. "It's our flagship product. It's had three terrific people guiding it since I've been here, and I root for Magellan as much as I root for my own fund. At Fidelity, we have a team spirit."

Who's the ideal investor in his own fund? "Someone conservative, who wants more income, who might be over 55 and not as interested in capital gains as someone of, say, 25."

What other career might he have been interested in? He reflects a while, then says, "This is what I've always wanted to do—since I was 12 or 13 and first started investing. I never thought of doing anything else."

The first stock he bought, as a teenager, was the next McDonald's— or so he thought. "I can't even remember the company's name now," he says with a laugh.

Mario J. Gabelli: Gabelli Asset Management

Asked to describe his investment discipline in 25 words or less, Mario (the Great) Gabelli offers: "Graham & Dodd plus Warren

Buffett." (Buffett, a student of Benjamin Graham, says he buys businesses, not stocks.)

Gabelli is a classic "value" investor, trying to buy stocks and other securities at bargain prices—for 50 or 60 cents on the dollar.

He studied at the Columbia Business School under Roger Murray, who edited the second edition of Benjamin Graham and David Dodd's *Fundamentals of Investing,* the bible of value investors.

To find stocks to buy, Gabelli first searches for companies with a "franchise," that have dominant positions in their markets. Such companies are more likely to survive downturns in the economy or in their industry, he reasons, and to emerge even stronger. He becomes intensely interested if such a company seems to be a bargain, selling below its private market value.

A good test of a company's value, as Gabelli sees it, is its earnings growth. He focuses on a company's free-cash flow, which he measures by looking at a company's earnings before depreciation, interest, and taxes (EBDITs) and minus required capital expenditures. Then he compares the free-cash flow to the price to check that he's buying a company for 40 percent to 50 percent off.

Next, he looks for a catalyst, something that will change investors' perceptions of the company. It's not enough to buy undervalued stocks, he maintains. You have to buy undervalued stocks that become less undervalued as other investors finally recognize your acuity and emulate you by buying shares. Gabelli calls it "surfacing the values."

A change might be a company spinoff of an unprofitable division . . . the appointment of a dynamic new manager . . . a more favorable regulatory climate (for a utility, or a bank, for instance) . . . or simply improving industry fundamentals.

The final test is the balance sheet. But Gabelli doesn't take the official book value at face value. He kicks the tires, looking for flaws that might throw everything off: Unfunded pension liabilities, environmental problems, and other skeletons in the closet. And only after applying all these tests does he consider buying.

There are thousands of good analysts on Wall Street who can read balance sheets, Gabelli observes, but only a few are adept at spotting trends that may change the value of a business.

Identifying those trends seems to be where Super Mario's genius lies. In the mid-1980s, when Congress began dropping hints that it would loosen the regulation of cable TV operators, Gabelli reasoned that pricing flexibility would lead to a big increase in revenues. He loaded up his portfolios with CATV companies—and made a killing.

His investment in Whitman Corp., a somewhat unfocused mini-conglomerate, was a bet that the new management would spin off one or more of its unrelated businesses, and that the sum of the company's parts would then be worth more than the company as a whole. When Whitman did spin off its Pet Food subsidiary to shareholders, within a year the price of the two stocks was double that of Gabelli's original investment.

Agricultural equipment had been in the doldrums for years. Farmers had overleveraged themselves in the 1970s; President Carter's decision not to sell grain to the former U.S.S.R. spread salt into their wounds. But Gabelli figured that farmers would finally be forced to replace their old tractors, so he seeded his portfolios with the stocks of agricultural equipment manufacturers, like John Deere. He reaped a bumper crop of profits.

A second-generation Italian-American, Gabelli grew up in the Bronx, NY, where his family was able to provide the necessities of life. His family was poor, he recalls, but lucky in not knowing that they were poor.

Long before he arrived at college, graduate school, and Wall Street, he says, he was a Ph.D.: poor, hungry, and driven. In staffing his firm, he looks for the same sort of people: People who will "sacrifice for success."

He became interested in investing in a curious way—by overhearing wealthy investors talk about stocks while he caddied at golf clubs in Westchester County. He bought his first stocks when he was 13; he helped finance his own education at graduate school by trading from a telephone booth on the Columbia campus.

Today, while his own portfolio is very much diversified, most of his personal wealth is invested in his own company's products. As the saying goes, he eats his own cooking.

Although Gabelli is known for his keen, quick mind and his audacity, he acknowledges that he makes mistakes. "I've bought my share of stocks that go down rather than up," he says, "and more than a few that did nothing." His more common mistake, he confesses, is not buying stocks that proceed to go up. His painstaking research—talking with management, talking with competitors, digesting financial reports—sometimes leaves him on the runway when a stock takes off.

Not surprisingly, Gabelli disdains index funds. Investing, he believes, should be guided by judgments about the merits of individual companies.

As for market timing, Gabelli doesn't touch it. Before the crash of 1987 he was fully invested, as is his habit, and his investments lost as much as the market did. But he is aware that the stock market makes its steepest climbs quickly, which is why he believes that it's more dangerous to be out of the market than to be in. In 1987, despite the crash, his funds rose about 9.3 percent, compared with the Standard & Poor's 5.3 percent.

And if you ask him directly whether he market-times or not, he gives a typical ironic Gabellian reply: "No. I'm not smart enough to market time."

Peter S. Hagerman: Hallmark Capital Management

A "quant" is someone who picks stocks entirely, or mainly, on the basis of mathematics. The opposite would be a "qual"—someone who uses qualitative rather than quantitative methods to choose securities.

Hagerman seems to be both a quant and a qual. In choosing stocks, he employs a mathematical system, but also believes that human judgment is a vital component of decision making.

He uses his own judgment to market-time, to decide when to load up on stocks and when to lighten up. Successful market timing is "frightfully difficult," he grants, but it can be done—"if you choose your spots."

The times to buy, he explains, are when the economic climate is "unacceptably bad" and to sell when the climate is "unsustainably good."

You can easily recognize the good times. "Everyone is employed. Everyone is buying a condo in Florida. You can't get reservations to fine restaurants later than 6 P.M., and their parking lots are packed with foreign yuppie cars."

You can readily recognize bad times, too. "Your neighbor has lost his job and, nine months later, he's still hanging around the house. If you advertise a job opening, instead of getting the usual 30 or 40 resumes, you get 600."

Still in his qualitative stock-picking mode, Hagerman takes heed of what products and services are popular.

"If my wife sings the praises of Liz Claiborne, saying that she can wear those outfits anywhere, I pay attention. I phone Liz Claiborne and ask for the annual report—and wind up reasonably amazed. I've marveled at McDonald's, too. The stores are clean, the product is good. And whenever I want something new, they produce—salads, chicken, breakfasts, whatever."

But it's unlikely that you're the first investor to discover superb companies, so their prices may be too expensive. That's where the quant takes over.

Using a computer, Hagerman screens 600 stocks for those with impressive financials—based on their earnings growth, ratio of debt to equity, and 10 other yardsticks. Then he adds a number, representing the stock's history, to the company's estimated percentage change in earnings for the next year. Finally, he divides by the estimated current price/earnings ratio. The resulting number indicates both how successful a company has been and how much of a bargain the price is.

Hagerman's advice: If you can't diversify among 15 or more stocks, or if you would rather spend your spare time watching the Giants play, stick with mutual funds. If you invest on your own, learn what a price/earnings ratio is. If you can't figure out what a price/earnings ratio is, stick to mutual funds. And always diversify: "I love McDonald's stock. But what if I'm wrong? What if the government suddenly outlaws hamburgers?"

Richard S. Huson: Crabbe-Huson Special

If you ask Richard S. Huson what the fund's managers are doing right, he gives a long, thoughtful answer—prefacing it with gentlemanly modesty about the role played by sheer luck.

To begin with, he explains, the Crabbe Huson funds practice contrarian investing—swimming against the tide. And the funds' readiness to buy fallen angels has proved a big advantage in recent years.

"I've been in the business 28 years," he says, "and it's only been in the last 8 or 10 years that you see these huge dips in stocks overnight. That provides a fertile ground for our type of investing. We look at everything on the way down. So many other investors concentrate on momentum—they don't look at anything not performing well. With us, whatever they're throwing out the window, we'll look at."

Why these enormous drops? Because huge mutual funds will boot out a stock on any disappointing news. "The drop won't affect the fund much, because it's so enormous," says Huson, "but it slaughters the stock. So the markets have given us lots of opportunities."

Beyond that, the Crabbe Huson managers do things a bit differently. "There are nuances in contrarian investing," Huson says hesitantly. And his firm tries to practice contrarianism as it was meant to be practiced: As a long-term philosophy. He invokes an analogy: "There are a lot of Dow theorists, but a few who actually understand it. Richard Russell [a newsletter editor] seems to understand it better than most. The trouble is, a lot of people call themselves Dow theorists who don't really understand it."

Still another edge their funds have: They study more than just the fundamentals. They're also into psychology. "When we're doing research, there are probably 4,000 other investors calling the same company and getting the same information," he points out. "Our edge is that we try evaluate how people will respond to any news."

That's why the ideal portfolio manager, Huson says, probably should have a B.A. in accounting, an M.A. in economics . . . and a Ph.D. in psychology.

Psychology means asking: "Who was buying a stock at the high? What was the story? Who's selling the stock? What's the story now? Who would buy the stock if it went lower? Are there people who will buy it from us—at a higher price? Those questions are always going through our minds."

Another key nuance: "We know what not to do," he says. Such as buying stocks simply because their prices have nosedived. He calls it "our price discipline."

They don't just buy stocks that have fallen down an elevator shaft. They buy stocks that seem likely to pick themselves up. You can buy a stock cheap and wait forever and a day for it to stop being cheap. "What you must do," Huson says, "is identify something in the fundamental or psychological picture that will change matters."

In the short run, investor perceptions influence stock prices, Huson maintains. In the long run, it's fundamentals. What his fund tries to do is get on the right side of the short-term trend by predicting how investors may respond to news about a company or an industry.

Still another advantage the Equity Fund has, according to Huson, is that it's managed by a team of three, of which he happens to be the chief investment officer. (Crabbe runs Special, which buys small-company stocks.) The Equity Fund has 50 stocks, and Huson himself manages about 15. The small slice that each studies "allows us to really focus on a stock," he says.

Each manager has the flexibility to create a portfolio within the portfolio: "We work together," he says, "but we can drift apart. Still, in our own ways we keep the contrarian philosophy flame."

There's a "good cross-fertilization of ideas," he goes on. Is there competition? Last year, all three managers came up with IBM as a stock to buy. Who bought it? "I won the toss," he says with a laugh.

Has any manager wanted to buy a stock another manager wanted to sell? Yes, a couple of times. One manager wants to sell, another thinks the stock will go higher, so he'll say, "I'll take it on." So, stocks have been transferred from one manager to another. "It's quite rare, though," Huson says, "because we're usually on the same wavelength."

Something else different is the 15 percent rule. If a manager's choice declined 15 percent from the purchase price, he loses control. One of the other two managers then must decide whether to hold on or to cut bait. "It's tough to sell a stock and admit you were wrong," says Huson. "This takes the burden off your shoulders."

All of the managers also have a lot of experience. "That's a positive overall," Huson says, "but it can be a negative. Older managers remember bear markets, and maybe they don't have enough moxie. It's the fear thing. Maybe we should hire a young kid to manage our fund when there's a bull market—he'll beat everyone head and shoulders." What about when the bull market is over? "Shoot the kid."

Jim Crabbe is even more contrarian than he is, Huson goes on, but all the managers share the same basic philosophy: "It's our way of life." But Crabbe, with Special, is in an unusual area—undervalued small caps. Many of them were once mid-caps, but they have fallen into the small-cap basement as their prices have tumbled. (For example, Mentor Graphics.) Most small-cap investors, of course, are looking for growing companies. "In a perfect world, so are we," says Huson. "But we are also willing to look at situations where there's less growth but the price is right."

Contrarian investing has its pitfalls, Huson warns. For example, a stock may fall from $50 to $25, but that doesn't mean it's cheap. It could just be less expensive. "The test whether it's cheap is how it trades compared to its historical fundamental characteristics," he says. "If a stock always trades in a range of one to two times book value, and if it falls to one times book, it may be time to take a look."

Another pitfall is the financial picture. This is especially hazardous in contrarian investing, when you may buy companies near death. Anything near death, after all, might just die. "We don't want basket cases," Huson says. He wants to see a decent cash flow, a decent balance sheet. "Most companies we buy are pretty solid," he emphasizes.

Still, contrarianism has its offsetting benefits. If a stock falls from $40 to $20, it's likely going to be less volatile if the market goes down —even though it's the same stock. "We call it the `compression beta,'" he says. And contrarianism tends to do well in almost all markets— and in all asset classes—except really hot bull markets, when fallen angels aren't what investors are lining up to buy. "We did terribly in the bull markets of '86 and '89," he admits.

While the funds were recently purchased by Prudential, they will remain the no-load funds they have been in the past, no doubt run in the same unusual, shrewd way they've been run in the past by the Crabbe Huson Company.

Warren J. Isabelle: Pioneer Capital Growth

Q. You're a growth investor?

A. We're not run like typical growth funds. We don't normally buy fast-growing companies with high price/earnings ratios. We think of our strategy as "aggressive value." We look at turnaround companies, for example—those that have taken a hit but deserve better.

Tokheim, for example, did everything wrong. It makes fuel-dispensing systems, and in the 1980s it was on the brink of bankruptcy. The balance sheet was atrocious. But it was the leading company in the area, it was upgrading existing systems, and it had excellent prospects overseas. We bought it when no one wanted to look at it, at about $9. It went to $15.

We don't buy growth unless it's clear that the growth hasn't been discounted in the price. It's rare that a little company has accelerating growth and no one has discovered it. But it can happen.

Take Analog Devices, which makes chips that translate analog signals into digital. We bought it although it wasn't in dire straits. It had already made a move, but it was clear that its earnings were accelerating.

Q. Do you choose sectors or stocks first?

A. We're stock pickers. We have a fairly large analytical staff, and we are a bottom-up fund. We don't look at sectors first. We'll invest in everything from shipbuilders to pharmaceuticals to pumps and valves. We invest in small to medium-sized stocks. We also like to concentrate our bets. We have fewer than 70 names in our portfolio.

Q. When do you sell?

A. Most funds are good at buying, but selling is what differentiates the good managers from the mediocre ones. Discipline is the key. To decide when to sell, we look at a stock's intrinsic value—the cost of capital, compared with the cash flow. It's as if we were buying a house. The cost of capital is what the mortgage would cost us. The question is, is the cost of capital less than the benefit of our owning the house?

Warren B. Lammert: Janus Mercury

Q. What is your strategy?

A. We seek earnings growth at a discount, wherever we can find it. We can be 40 percent overseas, and we have no market cap limitations.

Q. What has been your edge? Why has your fund done so well?

A. Over a short period, there's an element of luck. In the long run, you succeed by doing your homework, by really understanding the individual companies you are thinking of buying or that you already own.

I meet company management almost every day. And we do our own digging; we don't just rely on Wall Street.

We also benefit by maintaining discipline on the multiples we will pay. As the market rises, fewer companies tend to fall through our valuation sieve. We don't want to overpay for companies.

Also, our flexibility overseas helped. We've had significant positions in Europe since the fund began in May 1993, and our overseas choices have done well.

Finally, we are willing to hold cash when we cannot find stocks that we feel are compelling. When we sell a stock that we feel is fully valued, we don't automatically replace it.

William J. Lippman and Bruce C. Baughman: Franklin Balance Sheet

Theirs may be the only open-end fund that regularly buys closed-end funds, but it pays a price. Funds that buy other funds are allowed to have sales charges of no more than 1.5 percent. And with such a low sales charge, not many brokers are rushing to sell Franklin Balance Sheet Investment Fund.

The other fund that William Lippman and Bruce Baughman manage together, Franklin Rising Dividend, has a 4.5 percent sales charge—and far larger assets: $270 million compared with $110 million—even though it hasn't performed nearly so well.

But Lippman and Baughman, who work in Fort Lee, New Jersey, and not in San Mateo, California, with the other Franklin Funds, are full of surprises. One of them is that they think investors should be more interested in Rising Dividend than in Balance Sheet.

The recent unpopularity of growth stocks, they figure, means that Rising Dividend should soon begin enjoying its days in the sun. In fact, Baughman confessed that if he were writing an article about the funds, he would mention Rising Dividend before Balance Sheet. (Growth stocks have faltered, he believes, ever since Marlboro Friday, when Philip Morris lowered the price on its cigarettes. The word went out that big companies with name brands had lost their pricing power.)

Another surprise: In Balance Sheet, they're not putting much into closed-end funds. (These funds are really stocks and they sell on stock exchanges. The price per share may be more than the shares' underlying value—or, as is more common, less.) Normally, Lippman and Baughman put 25 to 66 percent of their assets into closed-ends. Now they're putting in about 10 percent: They don't think that closed-end funds are great bargains.

Lippman explains that closed-ends "accentuate the positive and the negative. You get double action. If the market is up, the prices of closed-end funds go up. The discount narrows, or the price goes to a premium. The reverse is true, too. If prices are down, the discounts widen."

Closed-ends present another problem. They tend to be rather small. "We put 2 percent of our funds into a stock if we like it, and 5 percent if we love it," says Lippman. "But 2 percent of our portfolio is $2 million, and we would be buying a big chunk of some closed-end funds."

Bargains are what they are looking for in Balance Sheet, even if not great bargains. A rival fund manager, also in New Jersey, is Michael Price, who runs the Mutual Series Funds, but they carefully distinguish between Price's strategy and their own.

"We both like buying stocks for 80 cents on the dollar," says Lippman, a wiry, intense, quick-thinking and quick-talking man. "But Price buys really distressed merchandise. Balance Sheet buys decent-quality stocks that are just out of favor. What he does, he does very well. But it's not what we do."

Adds Baughman with a smile, "Price's path and ours have crossed a couple of times." He was aware that Price's analysts were studying the same stocks he was scrutinizing.

Lippman and Baughman seek out underresearched stocks, stocks no one cares about. Stocks with low ratios of price to book value—and the book value must be tangible book, "not good will and other fluff," says Lippman.

They are perfectly willing to buck the crowd. "We don't care what Wall Street thinks of a company, or what investors think," says Lippman. "The question is, What do *we* think?"

Take Philip Morris. "It's still a growth company," says Lippman. "It still raises its dividends. Its total return for the past 12 months was 20 percent. Yet we're in the habit of apologizing for owning it!"

Half their day is spent looking at what they already own, the other half looking at new opportunities.

At Balance Sheet, they look for little-loved gems. "A company may be earning $3 a share for 10 years, and other investors turn up their noses: There's no growth," says Lippman. "We look at it and say, `Gosh, what a bonanza!' It's selling for below book value [the value of the assets per share], and adding $3 a share every year! The stock is becoming more and more valuable."

What will happen to such a stock? First, the market may recognize that the company deserves better and boost the price.

Second, the company may become an acquisition candidate because the price is so cheap. It's already happened to some of their holdings—like San Diego Financial, a West Coast bank. The book value was $300 a share. Balance Sheet bought it for $275 a share. It was acquired for $800 a share.

A third possibility: The market ignores the stock, but the book value keeps going up—thanks to that regular $3 a year earnings. So, after a while, the stock may still be selling at a 20 percent discount—but the book value is 50 percent higher.

What accounts for their success? Sticking with their discipline, they say. They don't market-time: "I've never been successful at predicting the direction of the market," says Lippman. "And even if I could predict it, I could be too early. I might predict that the market should go down, but it might continue going up for a year and a half. But whatever the market does, I can always find good values."

Lippman actually invented the strategy of buying funds with rising dividends—at Pilgrim MagnaCap. Rising dividends, of course, are a sign of a company's prosperity. But Lippman acknowledges that one cannot follow the strategy mechanically: A company may raise its dividends improvidently—or its prosperity may be the result of cost-cutting, not growth.

Baughman is a CPA who was studying bankruptcies before he discovered the pleasures of studying stocks for a mutual fund. He has the same fresh views that Lippman has. Asked why professional investors usually do better than amateurs, he replies that the amateurs become impatient too quickly and sell good stocks too soon.

"We have 80 names in our portfolio," he goes on. "That enables us to be patient. Every day, something is happening to two or three of our stocks."

Their research includes visiting companies, talking to the executives, and getting an understanding of the businesses. "I like to find out how management thinks," says Baughman. "We almost never buy a stock without talking to them. What are the problems? Are they fixable?"

While executives at big companies like Merck or General Electric may not be available for interviews, they make information readily available.

Lippman and Baughman don't like touting individual stocks. Recommending just one stock, they feel, is too dangerous. But under pressure they admit that they like UST Inc. in Greenwich, Connecticut, which makes smokeless tobacco—like snuff. "It's the perfect stock," says Baughman. "It's immensely profitable. The annual report will knock you out. If you wanted to make up a fantasy about a desirable stock, this would be it. It's presented on a silver platter."

Lippman, who is 69, was president of L.F. Rothschild Fund Management. In 1960, he founded the Pilgrim Group. Baughman is 45, and spent three years as an analyst at Pilgrim and was a portfolio manager with L.F Rothschild. Clearly, they have been working together a long time. Maybe that's one reason their shareholders have made out so well.

Terry Milberger: Security Equity

Q. You buy undervalued stocks as well as growth stocks?

A. Yes, that's why Security Equity is less volatile than most growth funds. Even though we're a growth fund, value issues slip into our portfolio, such as autos and chemicals. We're not wedded to any specific investment criteria. When we look for undervalued stocks, we also look for some sort of catalyst that will drive the price up.

As a growth manager, I tend to favor earnings momentum and surprises. Earning surprises seem to continue for a meaningful length of time.

Q. When do you sell?

A. As a stock works out, I get out. And if it's disappointing, I try to leave early. If the market has been doing well, but an individual stock is lagging, that's a red flag. Disappointing earnings versus expectations are another warning.

Q. How else is your fund different?

A. With the stock market so volatile, I've become more diversified. We now have 70 issues. None of them accounts for more than 2 percent of the portfolio.

Because we're so risk-averse, we'll never be number one among mutual funds. But our long-term record will be good.

Gary L. Pilgrim: PBHG Funds

Q. What's the secret of your fund's success?

A. We're a small-cap fund, and because we're so small we can take greater advantage of opportunities. Having a lot of money to invest can be a burden. But we'd be comfortable with $100 million.

Our strategy is to follow 400 companies and to use momentum indicators to find companies whose earnings are strong and that are accelerating. The earnings should be increasing at 20 to 40 percent a year for three, four, or five years, not just the latest quarter.

Q. Do you visit companies, or just go by the numbers?

A. We blend the two approaches. We visit companies, or they visit us, so we get to know them well. We have to know why a company is doing well. But we go mainly by the numbers. Knowledge of a company that's not doing well is of no value.

Q. Why did you drop your sales charge?

A. We felt it was in the best interests of current and future shareholders. I've never liked load funds myself, and I don't like 12b-1 fees, either.

Q. Where does the name "PBHG" come from?

A. The last names of the four original partners. I'm the P.

Michael F. Price: Mutual Series

You might think that growth managers are antsy and value managers are calm and relaxed. But Michael Price, a celebrated value manager, is full of energy. He talks fast, thinks fast, and moves fast. When a company he's bought into begins to disappoint him, for example, he's history.

Discussing the personality traits of a good money manager, he says, "You have to be able to pull the trigger. You can't hem and haw. You can't brood over what happened. If something doesn't work out, I'm gone." As he's said before, getting rid of your disappointments helps clear your mind.

Yet, ironically, Price runs a group of funds that require that he be patient—and that his shareholders share his patience. The Mutual Series group in Short Hills, New Jersey, concentrates on undervalued stocks, asset plays, even companies teetering on the brink of bankruptcy—or actually in bankruptcy. Waiting for these stocks, trading at a discount, to bounce back requires that you not get antsy.

He certainly can be patient. He arrived at the fund group in 1975, becoming a protégé of the legendary Max Heine. At that time a railroad, Florida East Coast, was in the portfolio. "It's still there," Price says. "It's still cheap." Sooner or later, other investors, he believes, will discover a cheap stock.

More evidence of his patience: For five years he's been considering investing in the Far East, via his new small-company fund, Mutual Discovery. He still hasn't gone ahead. "I like to stick my toe in the water first," he explains.

To a large extent, Price's investment success is due to his painstaking research: "We really kick the tires," he says.

"You can't just take what others tell you a company or an asset is worth," he stresses. "You have to get several measures of the value of its assets. In other words, you should do good work on the evaluation side, then wait for the market to give that stock to you cheaper. I think we do very good work on the evaluation side and on the market side— but that sometimes we pay too much."

In fact, when asked what his "edge" is, he replies: "Flows of information." It's not just his own analysts and outside analysts who keep him well informed. Because the funds are so big and have so much money (about $6.6 billion), any brokerages with large blocs of good securities for sale let Price know pretty quickly.

What would he like to have been if not a money manager? Ambassador to Argentina. "An interesting country," he says, "with interesting business operations." Or a teacher: "Teaching's really great. That's one of our society's big problems, the lack of science and math in our schools." One occupation that has no appeal is politics. "Everyone is always taking potshots at you."

He's not averse to talking about his mistakes. For example, he was on the board of Macy's when it was forced to declare bankruptcy. His most common mistake: A stock moves up in price, and he doesn't notice that it's no longer low-priced. "I may have bought it at $24 and it's now $36—and it should have been sold. I feel like such a jerk."

But he learns. "I should have been more involved in Macy's, instead of leaving everything to the chairman of the board," he says ruefully. And he's learned to check the prices of his holdings every day: "You can't sit still."

Despite his occasional mistakes, his record as a manager is superb. His older funds are up between 15 and 16 percent a year over the past 10 years. Discovery, in its shorter life, has done ever better.

Among Price's favorite success stories: In 1975 he checked out a stock on the New York Stock Exchange, International Mining. "I found that, unlike a lot of other mining companies, it was cheap," he recalls. "I talked to the officers, I talked to customers. All by myself, I figured it out, and I went on from there. I had learned how to buy cheaply."

What does he hope to be doing in 10 or 20 years? He's a contented person. "The same things," he says. "I don't expect that we'll be much bigger than we are now. I'll try to regulate our growth."

Douglas Ramos: New England Balanced Fund

Q. What's the case for balanced funds, those with both stocks and bonds?
A. I take a long-term perspective. If you don't want to deal with the asset-allocation decision, stick with balanced funds. Over time, they will pay respectable returns and with less risk than all-stock funds.

Q. What's your strategy?
A. We have a value approach, looking for stocks with low price/earnings ratios based on projected earnings. We also look for stocks with above-average earnings growth potential. A research team in Boston comes up with a list of 400 stocks, and we screen them for a mixture of low p/e stocks.

We also look for a high return on equity. We want our portfolio to have a current payout less than the market, so that the companies are plowing more money back into the business.

Brian C. Rogers: T. Rowe Price Equity Income

Q. What unites successful investors?
A. You need the courage—or maybe the stubbornness—to be consistent in your investment approach, to stick to one avenue. I've seen investors shift from high-yielding stocks to IPOs to growth stocks—and watched them crash and burn.

Q. What is your investment strategy?
A. We tend to look for stocks with yields close to or above average. We also look at how a company's yield has ranged over recent history, and identify companies where we can buy the yield stream inexpensively. When we bought Campbell Soup years ago, its yield was more than the S&P 500's. As its price went up, its yield went down, and we sold it. Recently its yield was at a discount to the market yield.

We like stocks that provide relatively high yields. We're also almost entirely bottom-up investors. We look at stocks on a case by case basis. We don't look into our crystal ball, decide that healthcare stocks in general will do fine, then find some companies.

Q. Do you market time?
A. In all candor, we don't make frequent moves. In my lifetime, I would have been better off staying fully invested in stocks all of the

time. Our range has been 55 to 80 percent in stocks. We're slight market timers—we wouldn't go to, say, zero percent in cash, or to 50 percent.

Eileen P. Rominger, Quest for Value Fund

Q. What is your investment strategy?

A. Ours is a value fund. We buy superior businesses, ones that have a high return on assets and excellent management, as well as really working for their shareholders. We also buy companies opportunistically, when their prices are low. Even a great company can be a terrible investment if you pay too high a price for it.

We analyze individual companies from the bottom up, and we meet the managements.

Q. What major lessons have you learned?

A. You really must know your companies. If you're not fully versed on what you own in a company, you might back away because of temporary bad news. Or you might not sell when the price reaches its target, and the stock becomes overpriced. We also like companies where the management plays on the same team with the shareholders. [The management owns stock.]

Q. Do women portfolio managers face special obstacles?

A. No, it's not particularly difficult for a woman. But to become a portfolio manager takes time. You need experience and a knowledge of the equity markets. More women will become portfolio managers as they build a base of experience.

What is rewarding about this work is that it's performance-oriented. You get a grade every day.

Robert J. Sanborn, Oakmark

Q. How many funds should someone own—besides Oakmark?

A. I talk to our shareholders, and my impression is that they own too many funds—9, 10, 11 equity funds. And because they overdiversify, they obtain only average results. In my own case, I have a long-term timeframe, so I'm 80 percent in Oakmark and 20 percent in Oakmark International, which is run with the same value-oriented philosophy. If I were my dad, who is in his 60s, I'd put half my money in a low-expense fixed-income fund, like one of Vanguard's, 40 percent in Oakmark, and 10 percent in International.

All in all, I think you just need three stock funds: one international and two domestic. One of the domestic funds might be value-oriented, and the other might be growth-oriented.

Q. What is your strategy?

A. The core of our style is not to lose much on the downside and to do well on the upside.

Here are excerpts from a speech Sanborn gave describing his strategy:

People ask me what explains our success. And I think that the answer is simple: We employ an intellectually coherent, time-tested investment philosophy with a competitive group of people in an open environment . . . The Oakmark Fund is an eclectic, valued-oriented, 100-percent no-load fund that invests in whatever sector—be it large-, medium-, or small-cap, or high-yield bonds, or foreign securities—meets our investment criteria. I believe that this flexibility is one of our greatest strengths . . .

We use five guidelines to invest the fund's assets:

1. Invest in securities at prices that are significantly less than long-term underlying value. We defined underlying value as what a rational businessperson would pay to own the entire enterprise if he or she understood it. We have a very long-term point of view, and frame the investment process as buying a piece of a business, not buying a piece of paper.

   If we are satisfied that a security is priced at a significant discount to its underlying value, our second guideline comes into play.

2. Invest with owner-oriented management. We look carefully at management's incentives, and we want management to own a lot of their company's stock. It is my experience that investment returns are enhanced if the interest of managements and shareholders are aligned. And when I think of our big winners, they are characterized by having managements that are among the smartest that we have encountered.

3. Think independently. We have an experienced, focused group of analysts in whom I have tremendous confidence. We get our ideas from in-house and from company contacts, not from Wall Street. I am happy to state that most of the Street firms that cover us consider us to be lousy customers.

4. Trade as infrequently as possible. Trading is an expense to the fund's shareholders—there are commissions, price impacts, and

capital gains. I anticipate that our philosophy will produce a turnover of 20–30 percent a year.

5. Do not overdiversify. The more securities one owns, the greater the likelihood of average performance, which is not acceptable to us. I hope to have the top 20 holdings represent at least 65 percent of the fund's holdings. The top 20 currently represent 71 percent of the fund's holdings.

That's a summary of the fund's investment philosophy. What I do not do is try to time the market, and we do not use derivatives and options, which in my view represent a cure for a disease that does not exist.

Peter C. Schliemann: Babson Enterprise

Q. What's your strategy?
A. We look for good, little-noticed stocks.

When people talk about small-cap stocks, they tend to think of emerging growth stocks—high-tech.

But the academic research showing that small-caps perform best is focused on New York Stock Exchange small-cap stocks, companies that have been around a long time. Those are the companies we're interested in.

The average company in our portfolio has been around for 40 years. They're still small-caps because they haven't grown consistently. We try to buy them in the accelerating stage of their cycle.

Looking for new companies is more difficult than what we do. Will they make it big or will they disappear? A high percentage disappear off the radar screen.

In general, we look for stocks earning below their normal profit margin, where we expect that they will soon return to their usual profitability. Most other investors will want to see an improvement first. We'll look at a company before it has begun improving.

Q. Do you look for a catalyst that will bring attention to a neglected stock?
A. Yes, and often it's new, more aggressive management. Maybe the company is in a phase where it's investing for the future, and that's temporarily hurting revenues. Sometimes an industry has been overwhelmed by intense competition.

Take Arctic Cat, which makes snowmobiles. In the 1970s, dozens of manufacturers began making snowmobiles. They were a fad. Then dozens of companies folded. Now only four of them are left, and they're not killing each other. The fad element is out. Snowmobiling is now a serious winter sport. And Arctic Cat has a ton of cash.

Q. Isn't there a danger that neglected stocks will remain neglected?

A. A good company's stock can stay neglected. That's probably the biggest problem we have—buying a stock too soon. Some of our stocks don't move during the first year. But if you wait to buy in, the stocks may move up too fast. We tend to buy and hold. Our turnover rate is less than 20 percent. That indicates that we hold onto a typical stock for five years. You need plenty of patience. And some stocks seem to stay neglected forever. Then, all of a sudden, they'll show a spurt of growth, and the rest of the investment world gets real interested.

Q. How do neglected stocks get recognized?

A. Analysts sitting in front of computers may recognize them. One of the most popular screens is good recent earnings growth, with a low multiple. That gets noticed pretty fast.

Q. What mistakes do even sophisticated investors make?

A. The biggest mistake we all make is getting too emotional. Falling in love with a stock and staying too long. You've got to divorce your emotions from the process, and it's very difficult to do. I don't fall in love with stocks, although I really like some. I'm fairly successful in not falling in love. I tend to get out too soon. When the rest of the world finally wants to buy my stock, I let them have it.

Sandra Shrewsbury: Piper Jaffray Emerging Growth

Q. Why has your fund been doing so well?

A. We're fairly well diversified across a lot of different industries, and a lot of different parts of the country, so we're able to minimize wide swings. On the other hand, we tend to have a regional bias: We're based in Minneapolis, and emphasize companies in the upper Midwest and in the Northeast. These are the areas we know best.

Still, our fund tends to remain fairly consistent.

Also, we don't market-time. We remain fully invested. And we're long-term oriented. Fund managers are under terrible pressure to be short-term oriented, but those who give in to such pressure may miss real opportunities.

Q. How do you find good small-company stocks?

A. We're top-down managers. We look at the big picture; we look for industries that we think will do well, then look for companies within those industries. We like to see good numbers, like growth rates at one and a half or two times the market in general. We use Piper Jaffray research as well as other Street research, read a lot, and talk to and meet with as many companies and analysts as possible.

Q. When do you sell?

A. If the story changes. But if the stock price drops and it seems to be just a blip, we'll probably stick with it or even buy more. We might also sell if a stock has done so well that it's become too large a portion of our portfolio.

Richard Strong: The Strong Funds

Q. Which of the Strong funds might do well now, in the spring of 1995?

A. Everything is cyclical, and it's time for growth stocks to do well. Growth stocks have been out of favor. This year, it's been only the big caps that have risen. Strong Discovery and Strong Growth may start to take off. I manage Discovery, and Ronald Ognar manages Strong Growth.

Q. Are you worried about the enormous popularity of mutual funds?

A. As long as the industry provides good investment returns, good services, and good recordkeeping, I'm not worried. Mutual funds have provided a valuable service for investors.

Q. You've been investing for 30 years. What lessons have you learned?

A. You have to go with good managements, managers who understand their products and services. You have to understand the companies you invest in and, if at all possible, invest when the stocks are correcting. You have to be patient. You have to put money to work for you, especially when the market is not making new highs. You've got to remember that everything is cyclical. Everything rotates.

Donald T. Yacktman: The Yacktman Fund

Q. Is your strategy at the Yacktman Fund the same that you used with Selected American Shares?

A. Yes, I'm still a value investor. Some people consider me more of a blend investor, emphasizing growth as well as value, but that's only because a lot of growth stocks end up as value stocks, and that's when I buy them. I have a three-part investment strategy, which is why our logo is a triangle: I like good businesses, shareholder-oriented, and selling at low prices.

Q. Why have you been so much more successful than other value managers?
A. What separates the men from the boys is that when good stocks go down, the boys don't view them as better buys. They get nervous and get scared out. With me, if lettuce is $1 a head, I don't buy it. If it's two for $1, I buy two. Other people turn the lettuce upside down and look for brown spots. Either you're a good shopper or you're not.

Good shoppers look for quality that's on sale. The average stock in the Dow Jones 30 varies by 50 percent in the course of a year. It may go from $30 to $45 or from $45 to $30. We prefer buying stocks at $30 rather than $45.

Q. What mistakes have you learned from?
A. This is a humbling business. You could always have done better—always bought cheaper or sold higher. Or you could have sold, and bought it back again cheaper before it went up again. And other people always seem to have done better. What I've learned is to stay with quality, and not pay too much attention to a stock because it's cheap.

Chapter 21

What's Wrong with Dollar-Cost Averaging

M otherhood, apple pie—and dollar-cost averaging (DCA). Yes, almost everyone loves the notion of dollar-cost averaging. Practicing it is another matter.

DCA means spreading your bets. Instead of investing a huge amount of money into stocks all at once, you invest a set amount every month, every three months, every six months—whatever. As it works out, you wind up paying less than you would if you had bought the stocks at their average prices because you bought more shares when prices were low.

The weakness of DCA is that few people follow it. When the market begins falling, when various pundits predict a long and vicious bear market, investors stop dollar-cost averaging . . . just when they probably should continue.

Why continue investing when the outlook seems gloomy?

- Because we might *not* have a bear market. The stock market, as a wit once said, will do whatever makes the greatest number of people look foolish. And bull markets start suddenly and make their greatest gains quickly.

- Because, as Sir John Templeton has noted, it's far worse to miss out on a bull market than to be clobbered by a bear market— simply because over the years the market goes up more than it goes down.

- Because the chief benefit of DCA is buying the most shares of stocks or mutual funds when they're cheap, not when they're expensive. That means buying stocks as they go down and down, not as they go up and up.

DCA doesn't necessarily work with investments other than stocks— with real estate, gold, and so forth. It works best with stocks because, over time, stocks wind up way up. And it works best with no-load mutual funds, where you pay no commission costs to buy regular amounts regularly. With stocks, of course, just reinvesting your dividends is a crude form of DCA—crude because the dividends may vary over time.

DCA is not for the faint of heart. But to quote Irwin Lainoff, who used to run the Neuberger & Berman Manhattan Fund, the way to make money in the stock market is to force yourself to keep buying— even when your brow is wet and your stomach is churning. Just when many other investors stop dollar-cost averaging.

How to Buy Stocks Cheap

Dollar-cost averaging lets you diversify the prices you pay for securities. As the example below shows, if you bought $2,000 worth of a mutual fund every three months and the price fluctuated, you might own 513.34 shares after a year, purchased for an average price of $15.58 per share. But if you paid $8,000 to buy shares when the price was at its average, you would have spent more—$17.50 per share— and accumulated fewer shares: 457.14.

	Dollar-Cost Averaging 513.34 shares			*Buying at the Average Price* 457.14 shares	
Date	Bought $2,000 worth of shares at	# of Shares	Date	Bought $8,000 worth of shares at	# of Shares
Jan.	$15/share	133.34	June	$17.50/share	457.14
April	$10/share	200.00			
Aug.	$25/share	80.00			
Dec.	$20/share	100.00			
Number of shares:		513.34	Number of shares		457.14
Average price per share:		**$15.58**	Average price per share:		**$17.50**

Actually, not everyone loves DCA. Two professors at Wright State University have written an article entitled "Lump Sum Beats Dollar-Cost Averaging" for the *Journal of Financial Planning*. They urge financial planners "to encourage their clients to invest in the stock market as soon as possible! Dollar-cost averaging is unlikely to produce superior results to lump-sum investing."

Let's look at the professors' methodology and their findings, then figure our how they arrived at such a silly conclusion.

The professors examined returns from the S&P 500 Stock Index and from 90-day Treasury bills (T-bills) from 1926 to 1991.

The "lump-sum strategy" assumed that a big chunk of change was invested in the stock market at the beginning of various 12-month periods. The DCA strategy assumed that the money was first invested in 90-day T-bills, then shifted every month into the S&P 500. Also checked were six-month and three-month holding periods.

The results for three cumulative time periods were then examined: 1926–91, 1950–91, and 1970–91.

For all three periods, the lump-sum strategy turned out to be better than the DCA strategy—from nearly two-thirds of the time to about 60 percent of the time.

A key mistake the professors made was assuming that investors sell at any old time. Not so. Most investors, I suspect, actually sell during the one-third or 40 percent of the time when DCA has beaten lump-sum investing—because the market has sunk into the pits. Investors typically sell when they need money—because they have been laid off from their jobs or their businesses are faltering. In other words, during a recession, when the market is (typically) down in the basement. And if investors are going to sell low, they better have bought low.

Another reason people sell when the market is down is psychological. They tend to panic when stocks plunge and to become euphoric when the market climbs. That's just what DCA is meant to prevent.

Still another mistake the professors made was not measuring how far behind lump-sum investing might ever trail DCA. With DCA, you're rarely going to lose much money. With lump-sum investing, you could lose an enormous amount quickly. And if you happen to need the money then . . .

Besides, how many people have portfolios as diversified as the S&P 500? Most people have a little of this, a little of that. Their portfolios are therefore likely to be very volatile—and to go down far more in a bear market than a nicely diversified portfolio like the S&P 500.

Anyway, the *Journal of Financial Planning* is a fine publication, and

I've decided to suggest some follow-up articles to the editor: "The Case for Buying High and Selling Low," "Collector Plates as Superior Investments," and "Why You Should Ask Your Physician for Investment Advice."

Appendix 1

An Introduction to Common Stocks

T his chapter is for beginners—or veterans who want to brush up on the elements of investing in the stock market.

Common stocks represent part ownership of a corporation, such as IBM, AT&T, or Coca-Cola. If a stock is selling for $20 a share and you want to buy 100 shares, it will cost you $2,000—in addition to the broker's commission (less than $100) and some other small charges. If you sell 100 shares, you should receive $2,000 (less the broker's commission and some other small charges).

Normally you buy and sell stocks through a stock exchange, like the New York or American Stock Exchange. If there is no formal place to trade, the stocks may be bought or sold through the National Association of Securities Dealers Automated Quotation System (NASDAQ), or "over-the-counter." Usually the stocks of bigger, sounder companies are traded on the New York Exchange, while the stocks of new, small companies are traded over-the-counter. But many large technology companies trade over-the-counter.

Normally you buy shares of a stock through a stockbroker. Some companies, notably Exxon, let you buy shares directly, bypassing stockbrokers. You can also buy shares indirectly through an investment company called a mutual fund. The fund buys the shares of the stock, and you can buy shares of those stocks through the investment company.

Some 10,000 stocks are publicly traded.

Blue chips are stocks of giant, high-quality companies, which usually pay fairly liberal dividends.

Cyclical stocks are those whose fortunes rise and fall with the economy itself—steel companies, auto companies, homebuilders.

Defensive stocks are those of companies that tend to hold their own even during a downturn in the economy: drug companies, companies that make soft drinks, food companies.

Interest-sensitive stocks—banks, utilities, and many of the cyclical companies—are dependent on what happens to interest rates in general.

A stock's price itself is rather meaningless, but companies that have been around a long time tend to have high-priced stocks, due simply to appreciation. Companies will "split" their shares, usually two for one, to lower their prices. A very low price—typically of so-called penny stocks—is typical of a small, growing company.

A share of stock is worth whatever someone is willing to sell it for and some other person is willing to pay.

Owners of common stocks can make profits in two ways: through the appreciation of the price of their stock and through receiving dividends, the regular payments that larger companies give to shareholders out of their earnings. Over the years, about 40 percent of the total return that investors reap from the stock market comes from dividends.

To figure out a stock's dividend yield, divide the amount of the yearly dividend by the current price per share. If a stock is trading at $50 a share and pays $3 a share annually, the dividend yield is 6 percent.

Stocks that pay relatively high dividends tend to be those of older companies, not growing very fast. Stocks of small, growing companies usually pay no dividends.

Shareholders who reinvest their dividends into more shares are in effect practicing a form of dollar-cost-averaging (see Chapter 21).

There are two basic kinds of stocks:

Common stock. Owners have the right to vote on important issues and to receive dividends resulting from the company's profits.

Preferred stocks. These are like bonds. The dividend rate remains fixed over long periods of time. Owners receive dividends before dividends are paid to owners of common stocks. If a company suspends its dividends, the dividends on preferred stock may accumulate. If a company goes out of business, owners of preferred stock are paid before owners of common stock. Owners of preferred stock also may not have the right to vote and the right to share in the company's profits.

RISK

While the stock market, over the years, has provided the best return on your money, there's a price that investors have had to pay: volatility. During some time periods, you can lose a lot of money.

The antidote to stock market volatility is patience. Data from Ibbotson Associates have found that stocks (from 1926 to the end of 1994) provided a profit in 49 out of 69 1-year periods—71 percent of the time. They made a profit in 58 out of 65 5-year periods—89 percent of the time. And they made a profit in 58 out of 60 10-year periods—97 percent of the time.

Compared to bonds and Treasury bills, stocks have performed better in 57 percent of the 1-year periods, in 74 percent of the 5-year periods, and in 82 percent of the 10-year periods.

As the chart below shows, if you had $10,000 invested entirely in the stock market from December 31, 1973 to December 31, 1994 (a total of 20 years), you would have wound up with 10 times as much: $110,351. If you had put your money in cash (Treasury bills), you would have less than half that: $42,428.

Now let's broaden the time period—from December 31, 1949 to December 31, 1993. During that time, your investment in stocks would have lost 26.5 percent in 1 year—and the average loss in 10 bad years would have been 9.6 percent. If you had $50,000 at the start of a year, you would have ended up with $36,750—a loss of $13,250. Could you have suffered that financial calamity without panicking?

Allocations			Average Annual Return	Best Year	Worst Year	Number of Down Years	Average Loss in Down Years	Value of $10,000 Starting 12/31/73
Stocks	Bonds	Cash						
0%	0%	100%	5.2%	14.7%	0.9%	0	NA	$42,428
40%	40%	20%	8.5%	26.8%	-7.2%	7	-3.0%	80,399
60%	30%	10%	9.9%	33.8%	-13.8%	8	-5.6%	92,151
80%	20%	0%	11.2%	43.5%	-20.3%	10	-7.1%	103,892
100%	0%	0%	12.3%	52.6%	-26.5%	10	-9.6%	110,351

Source: T. Rowe Price Associates, data from Ibbotson Associates. Based on performances for the Standard & Poor's 500 Stock Index, 30-day Treasury bills, and long-term government bonds. Figures assume that dividends are reinvested and the portfolio rebalanced every year.

With cash, though, you would never have lost a cent in any year. Your worst return in one year: 0.9 percent (because of inflation).

A sensible compromise would be 60 percent stocks, 30 percent bonds, and 10 percent cash equivalents. You would have wound up with $92,151, and your worst one-year loss would have been only 13.8 percent.

The true riskiness of a company is difficult to measure, but an approximation can be obtained from a stock's volatility. The prices of small-company stocks, stocks of companies in trouble, tend to bob up and down more dramatically than, say, the stocks of old-line public utilities.

One measure of a stock's volatility is its beta, a number that compares a stock price's ups and downs with the volatility of the Standard & Poor's 500 Stock Index. The index is given a beta of 1. A stock with a beta of 1.3, for example, is 30 percent more volatile than the S&P 500. Another measure of volatility is the "standard deviation," which indicates how much a stock's price has fluctuated around its average return.

ALLOCATING YOUR ASSETS
Most people should probably limit their exposure to the stock market. In other words, they should also own some bonds and some cash equivalents, some real estate and other tangible assets.

A key reason: It's easy to get worried and upset when you lose a little money in the stock market—or a *lot* of money. I recall, in 1974, talking with some fellow employees at Time Inc. about their retirement investments. The market over the previous two years had lost 48 percent of its value. In 1973, these people had had $200,000 in their pension plans. Now they had $104,000. They were white with shock. They had been planning to retire on their $200,000.

What's the most that anyone should have in the stock market? One wise investor once told me: 80 percent. "No one," he assured me, "is brave enough to keep more than 80 percent of his assets in stocks."

Another reason to limit your exposure to stocks is to stabilize your portfolio—just in case something totally unexpected happens and you must sell some of your holdings. (For example, you have a once-in-a-lifetime opportunity to buy into a business.) Bonds and cash equivalents can add stability to your portfolio. (Cash equivalents are any investment that's liquid and that comes due in a year or less: short-term CDs, money market funds, Treasury bills, passbook savings accounts.)

In only 5 of the last 68 years have stocks and bonds gone down together in the same year.

Cash equivalents may make you very little money, but at least they don't lose you any money.

A third reason: Bonds and cash equivalents sometimes do right well for themselves. In the inflationary 1970s, money market funds were paying 17 and 18 percent. Bonds did very well throughout the disinflationary 1980s, when interest rates began coming down, making existing bonds more valuable.

Just how much you should have in stocks, bonds, and cash depends on:

- Your age. The younger you are, the more you might have in the stock market. You have time to wait out bear markets. And if you lose money, you can always make more money to replenish that. Whereas if you're well along in years, you don't have all that much time to wait out a bear market or to replenish a horde of money that you've lost.

- Your sophistication. Are you so knowledgeable about investing that you can resist the temptation to sell when the market is temporarily going down?

- Your wealth. If you're not very well off, you may need more money for unexpected emergencies than your emergency fund has. If your Ford needs a new transmission, for example, you may be forced to sell a stock or mutual fund you own while it's temporarily low, just for the cash. Whereas if you're very well-to-do, you can just cut back here and there to come up with the cash you need. Not buy a new Mercedes, for instance.

- Your time horizon. If you're saving for your retirement in 15 years, you can be more daring in your investments than if you are saving to send your kids through college in 10 years or to buy a home in 5 years.

So, the younger you are, investment-wise, the farther off you expect to need the money, and the wealthier you are, the more your asset-allocation model can be tilted toward the stock market.

There's no one asset-allocation model clearly better than another. In fact, models devised by very clever people sometimes differ markedly from one another.

Below is a very conservative model, from the American Association of Individual Investors (AAII) in Chicago. ("Risk tolerance" means how likely or unlikely you are to panic and sell when the stock market declines.)

Risk Tolerance	Stocks	Bonds	Cash
Five years or more from retirement			
Conservative	40%	30%	30%
Aggressive	60%	30%	10%
Close to retirement			
Conservative	20%	50%	30%
Aggressive	40%	40%	20%
At retirement			
Conservative	0%	50%	50%
Aggressive	20%	50%	30%

Next, a simple and simple-minded model. You just take your age and subtract it from 100. That is supposedly how much you should be in stocks.

Age	Percentage in Stocks	Age	Percentage in Stocks
1	99%	60	40
10	90	70	30
20	80	80	20
30	70	90	10
40	60	100	0
50	50		

Once you've passed age 100, presumably you should sell the stock market short.

Now let's look at a much more aggressive model, which comes from *The Value Line Mutual Fund Survey*. The model provides a formula: 100 minus (0.80 × age) equals the percentage that you should have in stocks.

Age	Percentage in Stocks	Age	Percentage in Stocks
1	99.2%	60	52
10	92	70	44
20	84	80	36
30	76	90	28
40	68	100	20
50	60		

Notice that the AAII suggests that you be 20 percent in stocks if you're retired (age 65 and older, presumably) and you're an aggressive investor. Value Line, meanwhile, suggests that all investors 100 years old be 20 percent in stocks.

There's an even more aggressive model, which comes from *Worth* Magazine. Allocations don't change with an investor's age. Everyone should follow the same model.

Here it is:

Diversified stocks or mutual funds	50%
Growth stocks or mutual funds	25
Bonds/bond funds	25

Everyone, it seems, should be 75 percent in the stock market—even 100-year-olds. (How "diversified" stocks are distinguished from "growth" stocks is not explained.) Everyone should also be 25 percent in bonds.

Obviously, you should choose a model you're comfortable with, that seems to make the most sense to you. My only suggestion is that, after you decide how much you should be in stocks . . . make it a somewhat higher percentage.

Asset allocation models have two benefits:

- They let you know where you are and where you should be.

- Once your model becomes badly out of whack—because stocks have soared or sunk, or because bonds have soared or sunk—you will know it. And you'll have a chance to rebalance your portfolio, bringing it back to where you want to be. The best advice is to rebalance a portfolio not every three months or every year, but after a model becomes more than 10 percent out of whack. That way, you're buying low and selling high. When stocks or bonds have climbed, you cut back. When stocks or bonds have sunk, you buy more.

You should change your asset allocation as you grow older—unless you're investing your money for younger people, such as your children or grandchildren. A good time to cut back is when the stock market is going higher and higher, setting new records.

EVALUATING A STOCK

What is a stock worth? You can answer the question two ways: quantitatively (by the numbers) and qualitatively (looking at the real world). A low price/earnings ratio is a good quantitative sign; so are increasing earnings from year to year. A possible massive lawsuit against a company is a bad qualitative sign. Exciting new products are a good sign.

Here are some of the key "fundamentals" of stocks:

A stock's price/earnings ratio reveals how much money you are paying for a company's earnings. You divide the stock's price by its earnings per share outstanding. To interpret a stock's p/e ratio, or its multiple, you should compare the ratio with the stock's normal ratio, with the ratio of similar stocks in the same industry, and with the ratio of stocks in general.

Stocks with high ratios may be those of companies that are growing rapidly—or of companies whose earnings have taken a hit, but their prices have not come down much. (This is often true of cyclical companies, those whose sales depend on the economy.)

"Book value per share" is another measure of whether a stock is low-priced, high-priced, or medium-priced. You divide a company's net assets by the number of shares outstanding. It's what every shareholder might receive if a company paid all its bills, then went out of business. In 1982, the S&P 500 traded at 1.1 times book value. Now it trades at 2.6 times book, suggesting that the market in general is not undervalued.

"Return on assets" is net income (minus preferred-stock dividends) divided by average total assets. "Return on equity" is a company's net worth divided into its net income. Returns of 10 percent are considered good, and over 15 percent is excellent. These ratios suggest how effectively a company is investing its available money.

The soundness of a company depends in large part on how much debt it has, and how much equity. The debt to equity ratio is calculated by dividing total liabilities by total shareholders' equity. The "current ratio" measures relatively liquid assets a company has against debts due within a year. A current ratio of 1.5 is considered good, but it depends on the industry one is looking at.

Stocks Chosen by
the Panelists

Arthur Bonnel (Bonnel, Inc.): "A conservative buy-and-hold investor should buy an index fund that is similar to the Standard & Poor's 500. Put the fund away for 15 years and let management make the changes necessary to continue mirroring the 500. This gives the investor a diversified portfolio. This is for conservative investors only."

Rudy Carryl (MacKay Shields Financial Corp.): Green Tree Financial, Computer Associates, United Healthcare, U.S. Healthcare

Robert Christensen (Stein Roe & Farnham): Bristol-Myers Squibb (1), Emerson Electric (1), Enron, General Telephone, Meditrust, Minnesota Mining & Manufacturing (1), Plum Creek Timber, United Dominion Realty, UGI Corp., CPC International, Nationsbank

James P. Craig (Janus): Gillette, Wal-Mart (1), Progressive, Unum, Fannie Mae (1), Freddie Mac (1), Hercules, Coca-Cola (1), Bank of New York, First Data, Chubb, General Re, MCI Com. (1), Burlington Resources

Maureen Cullinane (Keystone Omega): General Electric (1), Wal-Mart (2), Motorola (1), Genentech, Chevron (1), Boeing, Disney, Fluor, AT&T (1), Schlumberger

Hugh Denison (Heartland Advisors): TCF Financial, Firstar, Norstar, Schult Homes, Pride Petroleum, Inter-Regional Finance, Thorn Apple Valley Farms, Marguette Electronics, CMAC Investment, Astec Industries, Toastmaster, Specialty Paperboard, United Wisconsin Services, Ryland Group

Richard Fentin (Fidelity Puritan): Blue chip stocks when cheap— General Electric (2), Dupont, Emerson Electric (2), Procter & Gamble, Colgate, Motorola (2), JP Morgan (1), Citicorp (1), Honeywell, etc.

Mario Gabelli: Tredegar, Nortek, AFC Cable Systems, Viacom, Time/Warner

Peter Hagerman (Hallmark Capital): McDonald's (1), H&R Block, Student Loan Marketing, General Electric (3), Minnesota Mining (2), Genuine Parts, Pitney Bowes, Dun & Bradstreet (1), Clorox, J.C. Penney, Anheuser-Busch, Ford, Harris, Rite Aid, MCI Communications (2), American Home Products, NICOR, American Express, Bausch & Lomb, Weyerhaeuser

Richard S. Huson (Crabbe Huson Group): IBM (1) ("As contrarians, we do not buy and hold. Each stock in our portfolio has a limited life, depending on how rapidly it swings from out-of-favor to the momentum buyer's favorite pick.")

Warren Isabelle (Pioneer Capital): Wilcox & Gibbs, Worldtex Inc., Allen Group, Avondale Inc., Whittaker Corp., Tokheim Corp., Acme Electric, Amresco, Carlisle Cos., Furon Co., Lamson & Sessions, Gehl Corp., NS Group, Inclone Systems, Microcom Inc.

Arnold Kaufman (Standard & Poor's The Outlook): Pfizer (1), Motorola (3), Microsoft, Emerson Electric (3), Seagram, Coca-Cola (2), Berkshire Hathaway, Federal Home Loan

Warren Lammert (Janus Mercury): no choices

William Lippman/Bruce Baughman (Franklin) no choices

Thomas Marsico (Janus 20): Merrill Lynch, Fannie Mae (2), Freddie Mac (2), Coca-Cola (3), Lowes, Citicorp (2), General Motors E (EDS) (1), First Bank Systems, General Electric (4), Browning Ferris, Allied Signal, Airtouch, Intel (1), Motorola (4)

Terry Milberger (Security Management): American Greetings, McDonald's (2), PET, MCI Commun. (3), Telecommunications Inc., Sherwin-Williams, Healthtrust

Gary Pilgrim (Pilgrim Baxter): Cognex, FTP Software, LAM Research, U.S. Robotics, Value Health

Michael Price (Mutual Series): Sears, Eastman Kodak

Douglas Ramos (Loomis Sayles): AT&T (2), General Electric (5), Intel (2), Sprint, American International Group, Fannie Mae (3)

Brian Rogers (T. Rowe Price): JP Morgan (2), Travelers, Sallie Mae, GTE, Pepsico (1), Dial, Cooper Industries, Marathon, Pacificorp, General Mills (1), Smithkline Beecham, Dun & Bradstreet (2)

Eileen Rominger (Quest for Value) no choices

Robert Sanborn (Oakmark): Philip Morris (1), Quaker Oats, American Home Products (2), American Income Holding

Peter C. Schliemann (David Babson): American Recreation Centers, Northern Cranberries, Walbro, Falcon Products, Brenco, Tennant, Toro, Raymond Corp.

Ralph L. Seger Jr. (NAIC Investors Advisory): no choices

Sandra Shrewsbury (Piper Capital Management): Motorola (5), Mobil, Norwest Corp., Minnesota Mining (3), McDonalds (3)

Richard Strong (Strong Funds): Citicorp (3), General Motors (2), Newmont Mining, Pepsico (2), Santa Fe Pacific, Xerox

Heiko H. Thieme (American Heritage): Merck(2), IBM (2), Philip Morris (2), Bethlehem Steel, General Electric (6), Deutsche Bank ADR, J.P. Morgan (3)

Peter Van Dyke (T. Rowe Price): Chevron (2), American Management Systems, Baltimore Gas & Electric, Rouse Co., Bell Atlantic, Citicorp (4), Union Pacific, Selective Insurance.

Donald Yacktman: Bristol-Myers (2), General Mills (2), Johnson & Johnson, Merck (3), Pfizer (2), Philip Morris (3), Ralston Purina, Tambrands, UST (2), United Asset Management

Index

About the Author

Warren Boroson has authored *The Ultimate Mutual Fund Guide, How to Buy a House with Nothing (or Little) Down* (with Martin Shenkman), and some 15 other books. Formerly of *Money* magazine, *Sylvia Porter's* magazine and *Medical Economics*, Boroson since 1995, has hosted a radio program, "All About Mutual Funds," on WEVD-AM in New York City. He also has written articles that have appeared in *The New York Times* magazine, *Reader's Digest, Consumer Reports, Better Homes and Gardens, TV Guide, Family Circle, Louis Rukeyser's Mutual Funds* newsletter, and elsewhere. A graduate of Columbia College in New York City, Boroson lives in Glen Rock, N.J.